MASONS

Employment law for the construction industry

Masons' guide

Michael Ryley and Edward Goodwyn

Christopher Dering, Consulting Editor

Thomas Telford

Published by Thomas Telford Publishing, Thomas Telford Ltd, 1 Heron Quay, London E14 4JD.
URL: http://www.t-telford.co.uk

Distributors for Thomas Telford books are
USA: ASCE Press, 1801 Alexander Bell Drive, Reston, VA 20191-4400, USA
Japan: Maruzen Co. Ltd, Book Department, 310 Nihonbashi 2-chome, Chuo-ku, Tokyo 103
Australia: DA Books and Journals, 648 Whitehorse Road, Mitcham 3132, Victoria

First published 2000

Also available from Thomas Telford Books
Masons's guide: Environmental law for the construction industry. Amanda Stubbs.
ISBN: 0 7277 2611 0
Masons's guide: Health and safety law for the construction industry. Susan Fink.
ISBN: 0 7277 2602 1

A catalogue record for this book is available from the British Library

ISBN: 0 7277 2882 2✔

Typeset by MHL Typesetting Ltd, Coventry
Printed and bound in Great Britain by MPG Books Ltd, Bodmin, Cornwall

Preface

The management of employment law issues has always been an important part of running any construction project. As employee rights are extended and as regulation increases, the significance of these issues is growing continually.

Employment law for the construction industry has been written as a guide for those working in the construction industry who have to deal with day-to-day employment issues and who need to be able to access quick, easy and practical advice. A multitude of general works have already been written which explain the principles of employment law and it is not our intention to add another. Our approach starts from the perspective that the range of employment issues specific to the construction industry, in which some 10% of the UK workforce is employed, justifies a book devoted to them alone. Therefore, we have confined ourselves to a discussion of the employment law issues which are of particular significance for the construction industry. In order to achieve our objective of keeping the book at a manageable length, we have had to omit coverage of many of the general employment law issues that are not specific to the industry, but which the employer in the construction industry may nevertheless, be expected to come across.

In an attempt to make the text more easily readable we have endeavoured to keep the text free of references and citations. For those who would like to explore the issues covered by the book in greater detail, the bibliography contains suggestions for further reading.

The law is stated as at 1 June 2000.

Biographies of the authors

Michael Ryley

Michael Ryley is a partner and Head of the Employment Group at Masons. He was educated at Bolton School and St John's College, Oxford. With the exception of a secondment to a firm of lawyers in Tokyo, he has spent his career to date in central London advising clients on all aspects of employment law and HR strategy.

Although he advises clients in relation to employment litigation, Michael spends the bulk of his time advising on the commercial aspects of employment law. He has a long-standing interest in the impact of business transfers on employees, a subject on which he has spoken and written extensively. Michael has considerable experience of acquisitions and disposals, both in the UK and internationally. With the growth of public and private sector outsourcing, Michael has become involved in many cases acting for both clients and contractors, advising on TUPE and its implications. Michael advises a number of construction companies in relation to their HR strategy, boardroom disputes the employment aspects of infrastructure projects and individual and collective dispute resolution.

Michael is a regular speaker at and chairman of seminars on employment law topics. He is the author of *Employment Law*

Aspects of Mergers and Acquisitions — a Practical Guide, Employment Law and Information Technology and many articles on employment law, particularly on the impact of TUPE on business transfers. He is a Contributing Editor of the Jordans/IPD *Employment Law Service*, a member of the CBI's Employee Relations Panel, and a member of the Editorial Board of *Facilities Management Legal Update*.

EDWARD GOODWYN

Edward is a Senior Associate in the Employment Group in Masons' London office. He was educated at Wellington College and Exeter University. Having joined Masons in 1992 as a trainee solicitor, Edward qualified as a solicitor in 1994. He has specialised exclusively in employment law since qualification.

Edward has principally been engaged in advising corporate and public sector clients on all aspects of employment law, both contentious and non-contentious. Edward has and continues to advise a large number of construction companies, contractors and sub-contractors alike. For example: Edward advises the Employment Affairs Committee of the Construction Confederation and has represented two consortia of contractor companies in relation to the clamp-down and introduction of the CIS. On the non-contentious side, this advice has included the drafting of company handbooks, HR policies, employment contracts and the protection of confidential information and customer contracts. He has accumulated considerable experience in outsourcing, mergers and acquisitions, PFI schemes and advising on TUPE-related issues.

On the contentious side, Edward has represented a number of construction companies in the Employment Tribunals, Employment Appeal Tribunal, High Court and Court of Appeal in relation to all aspects of employment disputes. This has included defending claims for unfair and wrongful dismissal, TUPE-related claims, equal pay, injunctive proceedings, disability, race and sex discrimination claims and more recently claims brought under the

Working Time Regulations and the Public Interest Disclosure Act. Edward is a regular contributor to *Construction News* and *Building*, and has written and presented numerous seminars and up-dates on many aspects of employment law. He is a member of the Employment Lawyers' Association and the Immigration Law Practitioners' Association.

CHRISTOPHER DERING

Chris joined Masons in 1989, after a period as a lecturer at Exeter College, Oxford, and has been a Partner in the firm since 1992. He moved from the London office to the Hong Kong office in 1998. He practices in the fields of construction, engineering and major projects and has been responsible for the firm's health and safety group.

In terms of construction experience, he has been involved in a wide variety of contentious and non-contentious matters, including in recent times the litigation surrounding the Channel Tunnel project, North Sea oil platform construction litigation and disputes arising out of major projects in South East Asia. He has also advised on land development (including land subject to heavy contamination), rail projects within Hong Kong and elsewhere in the Asia Pacific region and water concession projects in developing countries.

His health and safety experience has mainly been in relation to compliance issues within the construction industry.

Chris has lectured and written on many subjects both publicly and in-house, for Government organisations and others.

Chris is a former editor of the *Jersey Law Reports*, a contributor to *Service Level Agreements*, co-editor and co-author of *Eco-Management and Eco Auditing: Environmental Issues in Business*, consulting editor of the two companion volumes to the present (Health and safety law for the construction industry and Environmental law for the construction industry) and was a founder member of the editorial board of *Facilities Management Legal Update*.

Abbreviations

ACAS = Advisory, Conciliation and Arbitration Service
AEEU = Amalgamated Engineering and Electrical Union
B&CE = Building and Civil Engineering Group
B&CEJB = Building and Civil Engineering Joint Board
CAC = Central Arbitration Committee
CAS = Construction Apprentice Scheme
CIS = Construction Industry Scheme
CECCB = Civil Engineering Construction Conciliation Board
CIJC = Construction Industry Joint Council
CITB = Construction Industry Training Board
CORGI = Council for Registered Gas Installers
CSCS = Construction Skills Certification Scheme
EAT = Employment Appeal Tribunal
EETPU = Electrical, Electronic, Telecommunications and Plumbing Union
EICTB = Engineering Industry Construction Training Board
ERA = Employment Rights Act 1996
ETO = Economic technical or organisational
FCEC – Federation of Civil Engineering Contractors
HVAC = Heating, Ventilating, Air Conditioning Piping and Domestic Engineering Industry
HVCA = Heating and Ventilating Contractors' Association
JIB = Joint Industry Board

MSF = Manufacturing Science Finance
NAECI = National Agreement for the Engineering Construction Industry
NIC = National Insurance contributions
NJCBI = National Joint Council for Building Industry
NMW = National Minimum Wage
NVQ = National Vocational Qualification
PFI = Private Finance Initiative
PJC = Project Joint Council
SVQ = Scottish Vocational Qualification
TGWU = Transport and General Workers' Union
TUPE = Transfer of Undertakings (Protection of Employment) Regulations 1981
UCATT = Union of Construction, Allied Trades and Technicians

Contents

1

The structure of the employment relationship

1.1. INTRODUCTION

Recent years have seen a marked change in the pattern of employment within the construction industry. Particularly significant has been the decision of the Inland Revenue[1] to focus on the industry, which resulted in a considerable increase in the number of workers classified as 'employees'. As a consequence, a greater proportion of the industry's workforce is now covered by the employment protection laws and the degree of regulation of the working relationship has also increased. Additionally, the latter part of the 1990s was a period of steady increase in the enactment of employment related legislation. Most notable have been changes in the law at European Union level driven by developing social policy and these, together with changes made at Westminster, have provided workers in the industry with enhanced rights. As a result, the industry is facing the challenge of managing a workforce while subject to greater obligations and, at the same time, seeking to operate in a cost effective way within the industry's tight margins.

Until the introduction of the Construction Industry Tax Deduction Scheme (the 714 Scheme) in 1972, the industry had engaged its workforce on a largely transient basis. The fluctuating demand for

1

labour in the life cycle of a typical construction project and the nomadic nature of workers led to an industry which promoted 'casualisation'. The 714 Scheme introduced a degree of regulation in respect of workers on 'the lump', almost exclusively for tax collection purposes, and allowed a large part of the industry's workforce to remain transient and self-employed. However, in 1996 the industry had to reassess the way it engaged its workforce as a result of the Inland Revenue/Contributions Agency clamp-down. The final pieces in the clamp-down were put in place with the new Construction Industry Scheme (CIS)[2] which took effect on 1 August 1999.[3] The importance of this reclassification of the industry's workforce, whereby a substantially increased number of employees are now on construction companies' books, cannot be underestimated. Among its effects on construction companies have been the following:

- Companies have experienced a substantial increase in Class 1 Employer's National Insurance contributions.
- There has been an increase in construction companies' obligations to their workforces in that workers who are classified as employees are now entitled to more extensive rights than they were when self-employed. For example, employees enjoy the following rights which would not apply to the self-employed
  - ɔ redundancy payments and the right not to be unfairly dismissed
  - ɔ paid holiday under the Working Time Regulations 1998
  - ɔ the minimum wage
  - ɔ statutory sick and maternity pay
  - ɔ protection from unlawful deductions from their pay.

- Companies have lost some of their ability to be flexible in reacting to market pressures in their use of a transient workforce as a greater proportion of the workforce is now committed to a sole employer.
  These additional employment rights have added to construction companies' labour costs and have increased the importance of effective human resources management.

- On the positive side, companies have gained some protection in terms of securing their workforce in the event of a skill shortage in the labour market. By placing their workers on their books as employees, companies have been able to increase training opportunities and employee retention by building up goodwill and by providing incentives to longer-term employment such as pension scheme membership

1.2. Sources of Employment Law within the industry

The rights and obligations of employees derive from four principal sources

(*a*) individual contracts
(*b*) statutory rights and obligations
(*c*) collective agreements
(*d*) European law.

1.2.1. Individual contracts

It is often assumed by employers in the industry that when an employee does not have a written contract of employment, the employer is not bound by any obligations to the employee. This is not the case. A court is likely to identify a contract of employment from the fact that a wage/work bargain has been agreed between employer and employee. Contracts may be oral or written. Where contracts are silent on any given term of employment a court may be prepared to imply a term. For example, where a contract is silent on the length of notice required to terminate the contract, a court will generally imply a term to the effect that the contract is terminable upon reasonable notice and will evaluate what is reasonable in each case.

Where there appears at first sight to be no written contract at all, a court may be prepared to identify a contract from the existence of a relationship whereby work is undertaken in exchange for payment, deriving the terms of that contract largely from how the relationship operates in practice. Terms may also be derived from custom and practice, where the habitual practice of the employer gives rise to a reasonable expectation on the part of employees that the employer will follow a similar practice in future. For example, where an employee with no written contract has received overtime payments at double time for working on site on Sundays, he could expect a court to imply such a term to force his employer to make similar double time payments in the future.

Additionally, the courts recognise that certain terms are essential to the relationship of employer and employee, regardless of whether these have been the subject of express agreement in the employment contract. These include duties on the part of the employee of

- fidelity
- obedience
- working with due diligence and care
- trust and confidence

and duties on the part of the employer

- of trust and confidence
- to provide a safe place of work/safe system of work.

Under English law there is no obligation for a contract of employment to be reduced to writing. However, certainty is greatly assisted by doing so. Moreover, there is a statutory obligation on an employer to provide an employee with a written statement of certain terms and conditions of employment not later than two months after the beginning of the employment.[4] The terms which must be included are set out in the accompanying box.

Chapter 3 contains two examples of pro forma written particulars prepared for employees whose terms and conditions are determined by two of the industry's main collective agreements.

It is apparent that there are many rights and obligations which might be expected to arise in connection with employment

Statutory written particulars of employment

The following particulars must be given to all employees in writing no later than two months from the employee's start of employment

- name of employee
- name of employer
- job title or description
- commencement date of employment
- commencement date of continuous employment
- details of pay with method and frequency of payment
- hours of work
- place of work or, if mobile, the employer's address
- sickness or injury terms, including sick pay
- pension terms and conditions and whether a contracting out certificate is in force
- period of notice
- holiday entitlements and holiday pay
- reference to grievance and disciplinary procedures
- particulars of any applicable collective agreement that directly affect the terms and conditions of employment
- details of work, pay, length of time for work outside the UK
- if the job is not permanent, an indication of when it will end.

relationships that fall outside the scope of the statutory statement of written particulars, especially those terms and conditions which are likely to be of benefit to the employer. Employers are well advised to provide their employees with written contracts that incorporate those terms which must be set out in writing to comply with the statutory minimum, but which also contain a more comprehensive set of terms and conditions, taking the opportunity to build in appropriate rights.

1.2.2. *Statutory rights and obligations*

These include Acts of Parliament and Statutory Instruments which regulate the employment contract, often superseding contractual rights. For example, employees may acquire the right to receive a redundancy payment regardless of the fact that no such provision is made in the contract agreed between the employer and the employee. Notwithstanding that the employer and the employee have agreed a short notice period to reflect both parties' desire not to be bound to the other after completion on any particular site, this may be overridden by the statutory minimum period of notice. Increasingly, statutory regulation of the employment relationship is eroding the freedom of employers and employees to negotiate whatever terms of employment they wish. One of the most notable examples is the National Minimum Wage Act 1998, which came into force in April 1999. While the majority of workers in the industry are paid over the minimum wage (currently £3.60 per hour, to rise to £3.70 on 1 October 2000) due to the minimum pay rates collectively agreed through the various working rule agreements, the legislation will be relevant in some sectors where employers will have to ensure that their labourers, for example, are paid at/or over the minimum wage. The minimum wage is subject to increase over time in accordance with reviews by the Low Pay Commission.

The rights and obligations conferred by these various pieces of legislation depend, in many cases, on the status of the worker. The legislation is somewhat inconsistent as to whether rights and obligations are conferred on 'employees', those who operate under a 'contract of service', 'workers', those who 'undertake personal services' or those 'in business on their own account'. For these purposes, the assessment of whether a brickie who has been working on site for six months until completion is an employee, in business on his own account, or a worker undertaking personal services is extremely difficult and yet is crucial to understanding the rights which he has and the duties owed to him. In general, rights conferred by the relevant legislation will always apply to employees and to a much lesser extent non-employees. Although the coverage of statutory rights is increasingly being extended to a broader category of workers, the distinction between who is and who is not an employee is nevertheless of fundamental importance to the industry.

1.2.3. Collective agreements

Terms and conditions may be agreed on a collective basis whereby the representatives of a group of employees (which may be defined by reference to their skills or their employer) meet to reach agreement with their employers. Many employers within the industry adhere to standard terms and conditions of employment which are the product of national level collective bargaining between employers' representatives and officials of recognised trade unions. These terms regulate each individual employment relationship within the scope of the collective agreement; in practice, they operate as a standard form employment contract.

The main collective agreements which relate to the industry[5] are discussed in Chapter 3. In many cases, wage rates and the terms and conditions of employment of workers in the industry are determined by these collective agreements. An employer's obligation to provide a written statement of terms and conditions of employment is satisfied by the employer referring the employee to the collective agreement which directly affects his terms and conditions, so long as the employee has a reasonable opportunity of reading the collective agreement in the course of his employment, or it has been otherwise made reasonably accessible to him in some other way. Nevertheless, it is common practice for the employee to be provided with a conventional statement of terms and conditions, some examples of which are contained in Chapter 3.

Generally, a collective agreement will establish the norm or standard for the terms and conditions of employment for workers within its scope. However, a collective agreement does not automatically bind or benefit an individual employee. The mere fact that an employee is a member of, say, UCATT, which may have been involved in the negotiation of a collective agreement that governs employees of a description into which the employee falls, does not give that employee an automatic right to benefit from the collective agreement. A route must be found whereby it can be said that the employer and the employee have elected to have the employment governed by the collective agreement.[6] The terms of the industry's collective agreements may be incorporated into individual contracts of employment either through an express provision of incorporation contained in the employee's contract, or through an implied term incorporating the agreement as a matter of custom and practice. In either case, the collective agreement will be incorporated notwithstanding that the particular employee may not approve of all the details which the unions have negotiated or may not even be a member of one of the relevant unions.

Generally, once the terms of a collective agreement are incorporated into an individual's contract, the relevant contractual terms are unaffected by the termination of the collective agreement. This issue has been very much in evidence following the demise of the Federation of Civil Engineering Contractors and the effect it had on the old Civil Engineering Construction Conciliation Board (CECCB) Working Rule Agreement, the Federation being one of the parties to the bargaining process. As a matter of law, the old CECCB Working Rule Agreement could no longer be validly negotiated each year by reason of the fact that one of the parties to the Agreement had ceased to exist. Employees with the CECCB Working Rule Agreement incorporated into their contracts of employment effectively had their terms frozen. Only by either agreeing to enter into another form of collective bargaining and working rule agreement, such as the Construction Industry Joint Council Working Rule Agreement, or by negotiating locally could their terms and conditions be changed.[7] Similarly, it will be a question of interpretation as to whether the true construction of an employment contract is that it incorporates the collective agreement which is for the time being in force. In such a case, agreed variations in the collective agreement at national level may be ineffective to alter the terms of the individual contract of employment. In the case of the industry's collective agreements, because pay rates are negotiated on an annual basis, it is usual to find that the collective agreement that is incorporated into individual contracts of employment is the one currently in force.

It must always be remembered that an employee can choose to negotiate his terms and conditions of employment with his employer on an individual basis rather than collectively. Just how feasible this is in practice will depend on local circumstances. It is the parties' (i.e. the employee's and the employer's) intentions that are critical in determining whether a collective agreement is to be incorporated.[8]

Collective bargaining and trade union recognition[9]

The right of recognition for trade unions is a highly political subject and the law in this area has varied depending on which political party is in power. The Labour Government under the leadership of Tony Blair pledged to reintroduce the compulsory recognition of trade unions.

As a consequence, employers in the industry who do not voluntarily recognise unions such as UCATT, GMB, Transport and General Workers' Union (TGWU) may have a duty imposed upon them to recognise and to engage in collective bargaining in respect of pay, hours and holidays.[10] Where there is a dispute concerning recognition, the Central Arbitration Committee (CAC) will be given power to grant or to deny recognition and to enforce collective bargaining where recognition has been granted. The statutory procedure for recognition provides a voluntary and a compulsory mechanism. The basic principles are set out in Table 1.

1.2.4. European Law

Directives issued by the European Union may impact on the employment relationship either directly (in the public sector) or otherwise indirectly in that Member States will be obliged to enact

Table 1. Main issues leading to union recognition

---

1. Trade union makes formal request for recognition to employer.
2. The employer has ten days to voluntarily agree the bargaining unit and that it will bargain collectively. If such agreement is reached, the employer and trade union have an additional 28 days to conduct negotiations as to the mechanisms for collective bargaining (this time limit can be further extended).
3. If the employer refuses to agree or the negotiations break down, the trade union can formally apply to the CAC to act as brokers to decide the appropriate bargaining unit and to decide whether a majority of workers in the bargaining unit support recognition. At this stage, the employer can apply to the Advisory Conciliation and Arbitration Service (ACAS) for their assistance in any voluntary negotiations, thereby effectively delaying the involvement of the CAC.
4. CAC initially has ten days to consider the validity of any application and to see whether it is admissible. In order to proceed, an application must, *inter alia*

   - be received by the employer
   - be made by a certified independent union
   - relate to an employer with 21 or more workers
   - be in the proper form and identifies the bargaining unit
   - be copied to the employer with any supporting documents
   - not cover any workers in respect of whom a union is already recognised
   - satisfy the CAC that at least 10% of the proposed bargaining unit are members of the union and that a majority of the workers are in favour of recognition
   - show that the unions will co-operate in collective bargaining
   - not be substantially the same as an application which the CAC has accepted within the previous three years.

5. If the above threshold test is satisfied, a further 28-day window is provided for the parties to agree the bargaining unit. The CAC may choose to extend this period.

   If no agreement on the bargaining unit is reached, the CAC must determine the bargaining unit within ten working days, taking into account the need for the bargaining unit to be compatible with effective management.
6. Once the bargaining unit has been established, the CAC must satisfy itself that the majority of workers in the bargaining unit are members of the union seeking recognition.

7. If the above is satisfied, the CAC shall issue a declaration of recognition without a ballot, unless

   - A 'significant number' of union members tell the CAC they oppose recognition, or
   - The CAC has doubts that a significant number of union members in the bargaining unit want recognition, or
   - The CAC thinks that the interests of good industrial relations require a ballot.

   If so, the matter goes to a secret ballot.
8. The ballot requires the support of a majority of those voting and 40% of those entitled to vote. Twenty days are allowed for the ballot to take place.
9. Granting or rejecting an application settles the issue of recognition for three years.
10. Once recognition is granted, CAC has the power to impose legally binding procedures for collective bargaining on the parties if they cannot agree procedures themselves.

---

legislation which incorporates the provisions of the directives into national law. Regard must be had to the judgements of the Court of Justice of the European Communities in the interpretation of directives.

The social policy of the European Union has spawned a considerable amount of legislation in recent years, the impact of which has been felt throughout the construction industry, notably through legislation on working time and on the transfer of undertakings.

The process of enacting legislation in Westminster to implement European Union directives has proved problematic. The resulting legislation has often proved difficult to interpret with consequent practical problems for the industry. One of the most notable examples of this is the Transfer of Undertakings (Protection of Employment) Regulations 1981 (TUPE)[11] which are notoriously difficult to apply in practice. For example, a contractor pricing a buildings maintenance contract on a retender is unlikely to be able to predict with certainty the employment consequences of winning the tender, including calculating precisely the employment related liabilities he may inherit. The courts have done little to clarify such

European Union-related legislation, TUPE being a notorious example once again, and where the Government has published written guidance in conjunction with the legislation this has often been of limited assistance. Indeed, the original guidance published in connection with the Working Time Regulations,[12] left as many questions unanswered as it solved and amendment was required as a consequence. As a result, on building sites across the country, a given legal requirement could be interpreted in different ways with no-one clear as to which is the definitive position.

Notes

1. and, prior to its incorporation within the Inland Revenue, of the then Contributions Agency of the Department of Social Security
2. discussed in greater detail in Chapter 4
3. although the Inland Revenue granted transitional arrangements delaying the enforcement of the CIS until 5 November 1999
4. Section 1, Employment Rights Act 1996 (ERA)
5. the Construction Industry Joint Council Working Rule Agreement, the National Agreement for the Engineering Construction Industry, the National Working Rules of the Joint Industry Board for the Electrical Contracting Industry and the National Agreement as to Working Rules for Operatives in the Heating, Ventilating, Air Conditioning, Piping and Domestic Engineering Industry
6. see *Clugstun Construction Ltd* v. *Taylor and others* per Mr Justice Burton
7. see *Clugstun Construction Ltd* v. *Taylor and others*
8. *Wall & Others* v. *Standard Telephones & Cables Ltd*
9. at the time of going to press, the Government's intention was to bring the statutory procedure where unions can be recognised for collective bargaining purposes came into force on 6 June 2000
10. Schedule 1 Employment Relations Act 1999
11. which are discussed in greater detail in Chapter 8
12. see Chapter 5

2

Status of the working relationship

In any assessment of rights and obligations in the workplace, the distinction between an employee and a worker who is self-employed is of paramount importance. This is a recurrent issue in the construction industry and therefore it is explored in some detail in this chapter.

Unfortunately, the distinction is unclear and, as a result, the determination of a worker's status has never been easy. In *Stevenson Jordan* v. *Harrison Ltd*, Lord Denning remarked:

> It is almost impossible to give a precise definition ... It is often easy to recognise a contract of service [employment contract] when you see it but it is difficult to say wherein the difference [between it and self-employed contractor status] lies.

2.1. WHY IS THE DISTINCTION IMPORTANT?

Many employment protection rights are only available to employees—hence, defining whether a given worker falls within the scope of these protections is determined by categorising the worker as an employee or otherwise. Moreover, courts will imply into a contract of employment various rights and duties which do not form a part of the relationship with other categories of worker. The distinction is also important in the context of vicarious liability. An employer will ordinarily be responsible for the wrongful acts of his employees in the course of their employment; conversely, a company will not usually be liable for the acts of a contractor. To illustrate the practical consequences of the distinction, some of the principal rights and obligations of employees and of self-employed contractors are contrasted in the accompanying boxes

Note, also, that there is no longer any distinction between the protection afforded to part-time and full-time employees.[1] If a worker is truly an employee the number of hours worked per week is not determinative of the extent of the rights which apply to him.

Rights of employees

- Statutory compensation rights on termination of work/ dismissal
- Right not to be unfairly dismissed and the right to a redundancy payment (subject to the necessary continuous service)
- Right to written particulars of employment terms
- Minimum periods of notice
- Guarantee payments
- Three months unpaid parental leave
- Right to equal pay for work of equal value
- Maternity rights
- Time off for trade union activities
- Full health and safety rights
- Statutory sick pay
- Right to be paid wages without unauthorised deductions
- In some cases, the right to benefit from collective agreements such as the various industry working rule agreements

---

Obligations of employees

- To comply with the employer's lawful orders
- To work with due diligence and to work faithfully
- To give the contractually agreed period of notice to terminate the employment
- To pay Schedule E income tax (tax will be withheld by the employer under PAYE)
- To pay Class 1 National Insurance contributions via the employer

Rights of self-employed contractors

- To benefit only from those entitlements that have been expressly agreed
- To a lesser extent than employees, to be provided with a safe place and safe system of work
- To be paid fees gross, free of deduction

Obligations of contractors

- To comply only with contractual obligations that have been expressly agreed
- To work with skill and diligence
- To pay income tax under Schedule D
- To pay Class 2 and Class 4 self-employed National Insurance contributions

2.2. EMPLOYEE OR CONTRACTOR?

Surprisingly, there is no statutory definition of an 'employee'. As a result, it is necessary to turn as a guide to previous judgements of the courts when distinguishing between employees and other workers. Uncertainty concerning the precise extent of the definition of an employee has spawned literally hundreds of cases on this subject. However, despite this long history, there is still no definitive test which can be used in all cases to determine whether or not a worker is an employee or a contractor. Moreover, a number of the decisions of the courts appear to conflict.

The following practical guidelines are suggested in the light of the uncertainty as to the exact scope of the term 'employee'.

- Place all employees and contractors on contracts to formalise the relationship and to reflect the differences in the way in which employees and contractors are engaged.
- In contractors' contracts, expressly provide that the employer is under no obligation to provide work and, similarly, that the contractors are under no obligation to accept work.
- Ensure that contractors are neither entitled to sick pay, holiday pay or to bring a grievance under any grievance procedure, nor are they subject to disciplinary action.
- Ensure and, if possible, record that both the employer's and the contractors' intentions were to enter into a relationship of employer and contractor, not one of employer/employee.
- Pay employees through the payroll but pay the contractors on receipt of an invoice. If possible, do not pay contractors an hourly rate — but a fixed price.
- Place some financial risk on the contractor — either a penalty for late or unsatisfactory work or an incentive if work is completed on time.
- Only provide tools and plant to employees — require contractors to provide their own.
- While contractors are on site, allow them to control how they work as far as possible and reflect this autonomy in their contracts.
- Make sure your contractors take out their own public liability insurance.

Over the years the courts have suggested a number of tests to determine employee status. These are explained below and general conclusions are then drawn.

2.2.1. The control test

Early cases placed great emphasis on the employer's right to exercise control over what, how, when and where a worker was to work. The greater the degree of control, the greater the likelihood that the worker was an employee.

More recently, the courts have taken the view that control of itself is insufficient to determine status, particularly where highly skilled workers are involved. Although many manual workers in the industry will be subject to a high degree of control and will clearly be employees, it will often be completely impracticable for an employer to tell a more qualified person how and when to perform their duties. However, this does not mean that the worker is not an employee.

Control is now seen merely as one of the factors to take into account in determining the question of employment status; an important factor but not one which is determinative. Other factors must be taken into account as well. For example, in one of the leading cases in this area, *Ready-Mixed Concrete (South East) Ltd* v. *Minister of Pensions and National Insurance*, Ready-Mixed Concrete exercised a high degree of control over a lorry driver but he was held to be self-employed. He was not required to drive the lorry personally and could arrange for a substitute driver to take his place. This was held to be inconsistent with the status of an employee and consistent with a contractor's status.

2.2.2. The integration test

In many ways this test arose out of the inadequacies of the control test. The question to be asked is whether the worker or the work done forms an integral part of the business to which it is being supplied. It assumes that a contractor is usually engaged for a specific job to provide a service, whereas an employee is integrated into the main business of the employer.

The test has been of specific use in reviewing the status of professional and skilled employees. For example a surgeon, being a highly skilled worker, was not subject to the 'control' of a hospital but the hospital was vicariously liable for his acts because he was an integral part of the hospital organisation and was held to be an employee.[2]

2.2.3. *The economic reality test*

This test asks whether the worker is in business on his or her own account.

In the leading case of *Market Investigations Ltd* v. *Minister of Social Security*, the question was whether market research workers were employees. They were part-time interviewers for a market research organisation producing market surveys. Each survey was carried out for a separate fee. The research workers were free to accept or to reject work, to fix their own hours, and to undertake work for other organisations. They were not subject to direct supervision. They did not get holiday or sick pay. Despite these factors suggesting to the contrary, the Court concluded that these workers were in fact employees, because they were not in business on their own account.

A similar conclusion was reached in the Hong Kong case of *Lee* v. *Chung and Shun Shing Construction and Engineering Co. Ltd*, which also applied this test. Mr Lee was a stonemason. He was injured in an accident at work and claimed that he was an employee so as to benefit from the contractor's insurance policy. Mr Lee did not provide his own equipment or hire his own helpers. From time-to-time he worked for other contractors. He prioritised the work of the sub and main contractor when it was urgent. He had no responsibility for investment or management of the work on the construction site. He did not price the job. He was paid either for piece-work or on a daily rate. The Court said

> Taking all the foregoing considerations into account the picture emerges of a skilled artisan earning his living by working for more than one employer as an employee and not a small businessman venturing into business on his own account as an independent contractor with all its attendant risks.

This case confirms that a worker can work for more than one party and be an employee of one or all of them.

2.2.4. The multiple test

The multiple test involves an analysis of a check-list of factors which appear to point to employment status, balanced against factors which appear to point to self-employed status. This is a more appropriate test, in that it amalgamates the control, integration and economic reality tests, recognising that although each points to an important factor, no one factor is determinative. In the case of *Hall (HM Inspector of Taxes)* v. *Lorimer*, the Court warned against the use of a single factor to determine the status of the worker. The Court stated that all the factors should be taken into account and a picture painted from the accumulation of the detail. One should then stand back to consider the overall effect by looking at the detailed picture and taking a view. Not all the factors will be given equal weight or importance in any given situation. Every situation must be considered on its own facts.

This multiple test is the test currently favoured by the courts. It is, however, a rather vague test which can result in unpredictable judgements. At a practical level, it is difficult for the employer to apply in order to be able to determine conclusively whether he is engaging an employee or a subcontractor. The following cases are examples of the difficulties which the courts have had with the multiple test. It is appropriate to recognise that policy considerations have often had a large part to play in the outcome of a case — issues such as whether a worker should be able to rely on another's insurance policy. Such factors are particularly difficult for employers to be able to anticipate.[3]

In *Transmontana Coach Distributors Ltd* v. *Walker* the company advertised for a self-employed mechanic. Mr Walker applied. He was a motor engineer and had always been self-employed. Initially he was engaged on a part-time basis and two months later this was changed to full time. He invoiced the company weekly. His invoices said on them 'T Walker and Co.'. This relationship carried on for seven years during which time Mr Walker was responsible for his own income tax and National Insurance contributions. Despite letters from the Inland Revenue to the company's accountants to the effect that they were satisfied that Mr Walker was self-employed, the Court held that Mr Walker was an employee. The case is particularly relevant as it shows that neither the status of any worker for tax purposes nor the fact that he rendered invoices will necessarily be conclusive of whether he is an employee or a contractor for employment rights purposes.

In *Specialeyes (Optical Services) Ltd*, the company traded as optical retailers through a nationwide chain of shops, engaging a large number of self-employed opticians to carry out eye examinations. Most of them worked only for the company. They provided eye tests and took a fixed fee for each test. The opticians were held not to be employees. The company's degree of control was limited to deciding in which branch and on which day the optician would be given the opportunity to carry out sight tests. The Court found that the opticians were not 'part and parcel' of the company's organisation. They were contractors.

In *Filcom Ltd* v. *Ross* the company carried out telecommunications contract work for clients such as BT. In a written agreement, Mr Ross agreed to provide services to the company. In the contract, Mr Ross was described as a 'Contract Staff Member'. Mr Ross held a 714 certificate. His employment status became relevant when his contract was terminated for substandard work. Mr Ross claimed that the company had made unlawful deductions from his pay and the employment tribunal had to determine as a preliminary issue whether he was an employee. Despite the presence of the 714 certificate the tribunal noted that Mr Ross had been given specific tasks to do. He was responsible to a site agent. Quality checks were carried out on his work. His pay was negotiated according to a set scale. Although the 714 certificate was a factor pointing to self-employment, this was not the only consideration. The court decided that most of the contractual provisions pointed towards employee status.

The intentions of the parties and the label given to a worker regarding his status are also indicative, but not conclusive. The courts have often found it difficult to reconcile the intention of the parties and the label given to a worker with the policy considerations that underlie their decisions. Courts usually have limited regard to intentions and labels and will look behind any label where they feel that the label masks the reality of the situation.[4]

It is clear from the evolution of the various tests that certain factors are of considerable importance in establishing status without being determinative in themselves. It is necessary to consider the facts as against these important factors and then to stand back to judge the overall situation. Some of the most important factors which the courts have identified as being indicative of status are set out in Table 2.

2.3. THE INLAND REVENUE'S VIEW

A further complication arises from the fact that the status of the worker is relevant for a number of purposes and a different determination of the status of the worker may be reached for these different purposes. For example, the fact that the Inland Revenue has determined that a worker is self-employed for the purposes of tax collection does not necessarily mean that the worker cannot be an employee for the purposes of the employment protection rights.[5] It is interesting to compare the indicators that the Inland Revenue[6] has stated it will take into account in determining the status of workers (see box on p. 24).[7] The list is in no particular order, nor is it exhaustive. No single factor or group of factors is conclusive. However, it reflects those points upon which an Inland Revenue inspector will be focusing his attention.

The Inland Revenue's considerations are clearly angled at determining whether the worker is 'in business on his own account'. In this respect, the determination of the Inland Revenue

Table 2. Indicators that the courts have identified of employee and self-employment status

Indicators of employee status	Indicators of self-employment
General duties The employee is likely to have a job description/title and to be under a duty to follow the employer's instructions.	Duties and responsibilities are likely to be much more specific and generally will be spelled out in the contract.
Control The employee will be under a greater degree of control from his employer.	Generally, he would be expected to rely on his own initiative in carrying out tasks.
Equipment The employer is more likely to provide the equipment, including major pieces. Provision of small tools/equipment is not unusual.	More likely to provide the means to carry out the tasks including major pieces of equipment unless providing a labour skill only.
Time/Place of Work Regular/contractual hours more likely. Usually required to work on the employer's premises or as the employer directs. Likely also to be employed for longer periods (although short-term employment contracts are not necessarily inconsistent with employment status).	More likely to be able to choose hours of work. Not necessarily restricted as to workplace. However, contractual parameters for tasks/hours are not unusual. Less likely to have long-term contract (but long contracts not necessarily inconsistent).
Business/Organisation Likely to be an integral part of the business.	The individual is likely not to be an integral part of the business. Likely to be in business on his or her own account.
Personal Work The employee must carry out work personally and will usually be restricted from working for another employer. However, it is not inconsistent with employee status that an employee does work for more than one employer.	More likely to be free to provide an alternative worker to carry out the duties or to have assistance. More likely to have other sources of income. However, working for just one party is not necessarily inconsistent with contractor status.

Financial Risk

Little or no financial risk.	More likely to invest in management and provision of services. Often works on a fixed fee. More likely to risk loss and have the opportunity to profit.

PAYE/Administration

Will be salaried/paid a wage subject to Schedule E income tax, payable through the PAYE system and to Class 1 NICs. The employee makes no direct charge for services.	Likely to charge a fee for services and pay own Schedule D income tax, Class 2 and 4 National Insurance contributions and VAT. Likely to run own administration. Likely to invoice for services.

Employee Benefits

Entitled to holiday and sick pay and to enjoy insurance arrangements through the employer. Potentially paid overtime. Subject to disciplinary procedures.	Likely to make personal arrangements for insurance to cover inability to work. Subject to termination and damages claims only under the terms of the contract.

may well be open to challenge in the courts as being inconsistent with the case law, where the test of whether a worker is in business on his own account is only one factor to take into account in operating the multiple test.

2.4. MUTUALITY, CASUALS AND POLICY CONSIDERATIONS

One factor to be considered in the course of applying the multiple test which appears to merit particular consideration is 'mutuality of obligation'. The courts have consistently held that in order for a contract of employment to exist there must be mutual legally binding obligations between the worker and his employer. In short, the employer must be obliged to provide and to pay for work and the individual must be obliged to perform work. If there is no mutuality, there is no employment relationship. Cases in this category tend to turn on their own facts and the concept tends to

Indicators that the Inland Revenue have identified of employee status

- There is no risk of losing money in the job.
- Payment by the hour, day, week or month (especially unskilled workers). The Inland Revenue places particular emphasis on this.
- No separate business organisation (e.g. yard, materials and workers).
- Works personally (no right to provide substitute, hire help or subcontract out duties).
- Supplies only small tools — 'traditional and normal in the industry'.
- Employer has the right to control where, when and what the worker does. The Inland Revenue places particular emphasis on the existence of a foreman/supervisor.
- Worker provides labour only and is more likely to be unskilled.
- Worker uses plant/equipment which the employer has hired (especially drivers, lorries, demolition plant, etc.) The Inland Revenue places particular emphasis on this.
- Longer period of work indicates employment status. The position may gradually move from a contractor status to an employee status.
- Regular work for the same firm of contractors.
- Employer has right to move the worker from job-to-job as priorities change.
- Moves from site-to-site with the same firm of contractors
- Receives paid holidays/sick pay (especially long-term workers).
- Right to overtime.
- Contributions made to industry pension or sick-pay scheme. Participation in schemes such as the Building and Civil Engineering Template Scheme.
- Union dues deducted from pay.
- Worker becomes 'part and parcel' of the employer's business.

Indicators that the Inland Revenue have identified of self-employment status

- Provides materials or plant for job, especially expensive or heavy equipment.
- Worker bids for the job (especially through Compulsory Competitive Tendering).
- Takes risk of bid price being too low and risk of correcting faulty work at own cost.
- Fixed price work — same pay however long it takes. Worker may risk late completion. Therefore, analysis of basis of payment is important.
- Can hire others to pay as substitutes. Can subcontract work.
- Worker works for a large number of companies/firms in a year.
- More likely to be a skilled worker.
- Concurrently provides same work for others.
- Renders invoices for work carried out.
- Has own place of business to take orders and store materials/equipment.
- Controls own hours of work to fulfil contractual obligations.
- Higher degree of expenditure on the job.
- Enters the day-to-day transactions of 'a true risk-taking entrepreneur'.
- No overtime/sick pay/holiday pay.
- Paid by results (e.g. piece-worker) — but this will not always denote contractor status.
- Registered for VAT (where relevant).

---

be quite closely related to situations where the supply of work is intermittent.

The leading case of *O'Kelly* v. *Trust House Forte plc* involved waiters who were 'regular casuals' in a hotel. One group of workers was given preference in respect of the availability of work over other casuals. They sometimes worked longer hours than the recognised employees. They had no other regular employment and claimed they were employees of the company. However, there was no obligation on the hotel to provide work, nor were the casuals obliged to work when work was available. The Court of Appeal held that as there was no mutuality of obligation the casuals were not employees. The fact that the hotel gave preference to them did not amount to a legal obligation to offer them work nor were the casuals obliged to accept the work. Interestingly, the parties' intentions were held to be important. The Court of Appeal noted that the custom and practice in the hotel and catering industry was that casual workers were not considered to be employees working under a contract of employment and held that the parties could not have intended that the casuals were to have employee status.

Casual workers represent an important category of workers. They usually work for short periods with breaks in between when no work is either offered or carried out. They can sometimes be seasonal. Casual workers can usually also choose without penalty whether to come to work or not. The employer only pays for the hours worked. Casual workers often find it difficult to achieve employee status because of the potential absence of mutuality of obligations. Historically, the courts have been reluctant to find that a casual worker was an employee. This has been reinforced by the House of Lords' decision in *Carmichael* v. *National Power plc*, where it was found[8] that casuals who worked as tour guides at a power station on an 'as required' basis were not employees. The House of Lords held that the casuals' case

> founders on the rock of absence of mutuality, that is, when not working as guides, they were in no contractual relationship of any kind with the CEGB

The House of Lords confirmed that, to determine the employment status of the casuals, the following had to be considered

- the language used in the letters of engagement
- the way in which the relationship had been operated

- the evidence of the parties as to how the relationship had been understood.

As with the O'Kelly case, the parties' intentions were held to be important; it was accepted that both had intended for there to be a lack of mutuality of obligation and the House of Lords was not prepared to interfere with this intention. Interestingly, the House of Lords suggested that determination of the casuals' status could be undertaken solely on the basis of the letters of engagement if the parties 'intended them to constitute an exclusive memorial of their relationship'.[9] Similar relationships may be established under a 'zero hours contract' where the work is intended by both parties to be undertaken by employees but where the pattern of work is intermittent. There may be a fine line between employee and self-employed status in such cases and it is notable in the Carmichael case how the House of Lords and the Court of Appeal arrived at different conclusions on the same facts.

The case of Express & Echo Publications Ltd v. Tanton, which was heard before the House of Lords' hearing in Carmichael, echoes the importance of the parties' intentions and the terms of their contract. Here the Court of Appeal held that a worker whose contract specifically stated that he could arrange for another person to do the work for him was a subcontractor rather than an employee. The Court of Appeal, in reaching this decision, held that the employment tribunal had paid too much attention to how the contract was performed (in that, in practice, the worker had always undertaken the work himself) and not enough to the actual written terms. The cases of Express & Echo and Carmichael show the importance currently given by the courts to the contractual terms into which the parties have entered. However, the cases must be seen in context — these are borderline cases where the application of the multiple test proves inconclusive and factors such as the intentions of the parties tip the balance.

Policy decisions have been seen to influence the determination of status in many cases. The case of Lane v. Shire Roofing Co. (Oxford) Ltd is a good example which again serves to highlight the problem of distinguishing status where the parties themselves had been happy to consider the worker's engagement as self-employment for fiscal reasons. Mr Lane was a roofer who had traded as a one-man firm previously, but when work had dried up he started to work for others. When engaged by the defendant roofing contractor on a 'payment by job' basis, Mr Lane fell off a ladder and suffered serious brain damage. He brought a personal injury claim against the defendant roofing contractor in order to benefit from their employers' liability insurance. To succeed, he had to show that he was an employee; as a self-employed contractor he would not have been covered by the policy. Much as the result appeared surprising on its facts, the Court found him to be an employee and his claim was able to proceed. Two policy issues arise from the case

(a) Would the decision have been the same if the claim arose in the context of employment rights such as unfair dismissal rather than in such a severe personal injury claim? It appears that the Court in this case may have been swayed in reaching their finding so as to ensure that Mr Lane had some recourse and compensation for his injury.

(b) What would the likely reaction be of the Inland Revenue in relation to this new-found employment status as regards non-payment of Class 1 NIC and Schedule E Income Tax through PAYE?

In the course of his judgement in the *Lane* case, the Court[10] emphasised the need to take a broad view of the status of workers in order to ensure that proper insurance arrangements are in place.

> The overall employment background is very different today … First, for a variety of reasons there are more self-employed and fewer in employment. There is a greater flexibility in employment, with more temporary and shared employment. Second, there are perceived advantages for both workmen and employers in the relationship between them being that of independent contractor. From the workmen's point of view, being self-employed brings him into a more benevolent and less prompt taxation regime. From the employer's point of view, the protection of the employees' rights contained in the employment protection legislation of the 1970s

brought certain perceived disincentives to the employer to take on full-time long-term employees . . . . But, as I have already said, there were, and are, good policy reasons in the safety at work field to ensure that the law properly categorises between employees and independent contractors.

Clearly, the lack of any single test to indicate employee status is unsatisfactory in practical terms, but in some ways the position is inevitable. The important point is that it is dangerous merely to make assumptions about a worker's status without actually reviewing the facts that lie behind the relationship. In some respects the distinction between employees and other categories of worker is being eroded by legislation which uses different terminology when determining the type of worker who qualifies for the relevant statutory rights. For instance, under the Working Time Regulations 1998 a worker who provides 'personal work' qualifies for protection. A worker 'in business on his own account' is expressly excluded. Similarly, the definition used in the Minimum Wage legislation for the type of worker who will qualify for protection is

> an individual who has entered into or works under a contract of employment or any other contract whereby the individual undertakes to do or perform personally any work or services . . .

There is a general trend in recent legislation towards expanding the scope of the workers to whom such protection applies, as the proportion of the workforce who are not employees grows. This may further increase if the Government exercises its rights to pass further legislation expanding statutory protection previously provided only to employees to the wider category of workers.[11]

NOTES

1. The Part-time Workers (Prevention of Less Favourable Treatment) Regulations 2000 which are due to come into force on 1 July 2000.

2. *Cassidy* v. *Ministry of Health*
3. see further p. 27.
4. see *O'Kelly* v. *Trusthouse Forte plc*
5. see above *Transmontana Coach Distributors Ltd* v. *Walker*
6. and formerly the Contributions Agency
7. see Inland Revenue leaflets IR56/N139, IR148/CA69 and guidance on application of employment status rules to workers using intermediaries
8. overturning the Court of Appeal's majority decision
9. per Lord Irvine of Lairg LC
10. per Henry LJ
11. Section 23 of Employment Relations Act 1999 which allows the Secretary of State to introduce Regulations to make such changes

3

Collective bargaining agreements in the industry

3.1. INTRODUCTION

The terms and conditions of employment of a majority of employees employed in the construction industry are governed to a greater or lesser degree by a handful of industry-wide collective agreements. The scope of these various collective agreements correlate to the type of work involved. In some instances, there is the potential for overlap between the collective agreements (e.g. the terms relating to second tier productivity payments applicable to the heating and ventilating operatives engaged under the National Agreement for the Heating, Ventilating, Air Conditioning, Piping and Domestic Engineering Industry who work on a project that is 'nominated' by the National Joint Council for the Engineering Construction Industry). It is important for employers to clearly define which, if any, collective agreement is deemed to apply to their employees. It will only regulate the terms of employment of a given employee if the employer and the employee have agreed to be governed by the terms of the agreement. Whether or not the employee is a member of one of the unions involved in the collective bargaining forum is immaterial. As such, the incorporation of a collective agreement into an employee's contract of employment is best provided by written agreement, for example in a letter of engagement or a statement of particulars of employment.[1]

Employers are obliged to provide their employees with details of any collective agreement which directly affects the terms and conditions of their employment, together with details of the persons by whom the collective agreement was made. As discussed in Chapter 1, this obligation is satisfied by the employer referring the employee to the collective agreement itself, so long as the employee has a reasonable opportunity of reading the collective agreement in the course of his employment.

In this chapter, four collective agreements are considered, namely

- the Construction Industry Joint Council (CIJC) Working Rule Agreement
- the National Agreement for the Engineering Construction Industry
- the National Working Rules of the Joint Industry Board (JIB) for the Electrical Contracting Industry
- the National Agreement for the Heating, Ventilation, Air Conditioning, Piping and Domestic Engineering Industry.

The history and scope of each collective agreement are briefly considered and some of the more important or unusual aspects of the respective collective agreements are also discussed.

3.2. CONSTRUCTION INDUSTRY JOINT COUNCIL WORKING RULE AGREEMENT

The Construction Industry Joint Council Working Rule Agreement (CIJC Working Rule Agreement) was established for the first time by the Construction Industry Joint Council in January 1998 through negotiations by the Building and Civil Engineering Joint Negotiators Committee following the demise of the Civil

Engineering Construction Conciliation Board (CECCB). Prior to the CIJC Working Rule Agreement, terms and conditions for operatives within the civil engineering and building construction industry were set by two separate bodies, the CECCB and the National Joint Council for the Building Industry (NJCBI).

The CECCB Working Rule Agreement dealt with operatives' terms involved in civil engineering work, whilst the NJCBI Working Rule Agreement dealt with the terms and conditions of operatives involved in building work in the construction industry. Basic rates of pay for craftsmen, skilled and general operatives were the same under both agreements. Amendments to both the CECCB and NJCBI Working Rule Agreements were negotiated by a body called the Building and Civil Engineering Joint Board (B&CEJB) which consisted of

- Employers' representatives
  - Building Employers' Confederation[2]
  - Federation of Civil Engineering Contractors (FCEC)
- Trade unions
  - Union of Construction and Allied Trade Technicians (UCATT)
  - Transport and General Workers Union (TGWU)
  - General Municipal and Boilermakers' Union (GMB)

On completion of negotiations, the B&CEJB would recommend that the two constituent bodies (CECCB and NJCBI) should ratify and promulgate the agreement reached by the B&CEJB on basic rates of pay and allowances, into both working rule agreements. Amendments to the working rule agreements could only be made once the CECCB and NJCBI ratified the proposals.

In November 1996, the FCEC, one of the employer parties to the CECCB Working Rule Agreement, was dissolved by resolution of its council. In October/November 1996, a leading barrister advised that due to the withdrawal of the FCEC, the CECCB had effectively ceased to exist as the FCEC had provided representatives on the employer's side of the CECCB. This also meant that the existing CECCB Working Rule Agreement could not be altered or amended and that the CECCB ceased to have legal validity as an authoritative body over the CECCB Working Rule Agreement. It was recognised that some new negotiating machinery would need to be set up to provide collective agreements that reflected contemporary issues and rates of pay in the building and civil engineering industry.

As a result, the Building and Civil Engineering Joint Negotiators Committee was established. It had no constitutional or legal right to amend either of the existing working rule agreements, but it could make recommendations. It was this body that took charge of negotiations to establish a new authoritative body and a new working rule agreement.

Eventually, on 4 December 1997, the Building and Civil Engineering Joint Negotiators Committee reached agreement in respect of an increase in the rate of pay of those operatives employed under the then existing NJCBI and CECCB Working Rule Agreements for the year 1997/1998. While there was a question mark as to whether the CECCB and the NJCBI could ratify or promulgate this agreed increase in rate of pay, the increase was put forward to the NJCBI and CECCB member employers. Thereafter, on 1 January 1998 the CIJC was established, with a new national collective agreement (the CIJC Working Rule Agreement) being agreed to cover both the building and civil engineering sides of the construction industry with effect from 29 June 1998.

The 'Adherent Bodies' to the CIJC and the CIJC Working Rule Agreement are:

- Employers' representatives
  - Construction Confederation[3]
  - National Federation of Roofing Contractors
  - National Association of Shopfitters
- Trade unions
  - UCATT
  - TGWU
  - GMB.

The aims and functions of the CIJC are stated at Working Rule 6 of the CIJC Working Rule Agreement to be as follows

- To agree rates of wages and other emoluments of building and civil engineering operatives.
- To agree terms and conditions of employment for building and civil engineering operatives and to publish them as working rules for the building and civil engineering industry.
- To deal with disputes or differences involving or likely to involve any member or members of an adherent body to this agreement in accordance with the conciliation procedure.
- To consider proposals for, and to make amendments to, the Working Rules.
- At the request of either side of the CIJC to consider any industrial or economic question which has or is likely to have a bearing on industrial relations in the building and civil engineering industry.
- To take all reasonably practicable steps to ensure that operatives are employed under the Working Rule Agreement.

Unlike the National Agreement for the Engineering Construction Industry, the scope of the CIJC Working Rule Agreement is rather ambiguous. The agreement does not make it clear whether it affects employees or workers or subcontractors. Working Rule 1 refers to those 'operatives employed to carry out work in the Building and Civil Engineering Industry'. The guidance notes to the Working Rules state that it is the intention of all the parties that 'operatives employed in the Building and Civil Engineering Industry are engaged under the terms and conditions of the CIJC Working Rule Agreement'.

While the CIJC Working Rule Agreement sets out minimum industry rates of standard pay, the payment of bonuses is left expressly for agreement locally. To this extent, the CIJC Working Rule Agreement differs from other industry collective agreements.

In line with the CIJC's aim to settle disputes and differences, the CIJC Working Rule Agreement provides for a conciliation procedure in case of disputes. Furthermore strikes, lockouts or

CONSTRUCTION INDUSTRY JOINT COUNCIL
STATEMENT
OF PARTICULARS OF MAIN TERMS OF EMPLOYMENT

All the provisions of the Construction Industry Joint Council (CIJC) Working Rule Agreement (WRA) whether expressly referred to or not, form part of your terms and conditions of employment and should be read in conjunction with this statement. A copy of the CIJC Working Rule Agreement is available for inspection at ....

Date of issue of statement ....

1a   Name of Employer ....
1b   Employer'sAddress..
1c   Place of Work (if different from 1b above and/or variable)   ....
    At any time during your employment you may be transferred from one job or site to another job or site subject to Working Rule 14.

2   Name of Employee:..Job Title .... Working Rule 17.3.
    The job title is not definitive, you may be required to carry out alternative work from time to time.

3   You have/have not had* employment which, counts as continuous with your current employment. Accordingly, your period of
    continuous employment began on ....

4   Your remuneration is paid by weekly instalments in arrears.
    On the date of issue of this statement your rate of pay was .... per hour in accordance with Working Rule 1.
    (£.................... per 39 hour week) with other payments as specified ....

5   Your hours are 39 hours per week in accordance with Working Rule 3: Monday to Thursday from ....to
    .... Fridays from .... to .... You are entitled to rest breaks, not exceeding one hour
    per day in accordance with Working Rule 3.1 NB Rests breaks do not form part of the normal working hours.

6   Where work is temporarily stopped or not provided by the Employer you may be temporarily laid off in accordance with
    Working Rule 17.4.

7   Overtime, which must be authorised, is calculated on a daily basis. You may not unreasonably refuse to work overtime when
    required.
    Overtime payments will be in accordance with Working Rule 4 and where there has been no unauthorised absence in the relevant
    week, shall be calculated as follows:
    Monday to Friday – first four hours after completion of normal working hours for the day: time and a half; thereafter until
    starting time next morning: double time.
    Saturday – first four hours: time and a half: thereafter double time.
    Sunday – double time until starting time on Monday.

36

8   Annual Holidays — you are entitled to 21 days holiday – 7 working days must be taken in conjunction with Christmas Day, Boxing Day and New Years Day and 4 working days must be taken immediately following Easter Monday; the remaining 10 days are to be taken by mutual agreement with your employer between 1 April to and 30 September of each year – in accordance with Working Rule 18.

Payments for holidays are determined by the number and value of weekly holiday credits vested with the Building & Civil Engineering Holidays with Pay Management Company. On termination of employment you are entitled to receive a statement setting out the total value of your weekly holiday credits. The weekly holiday credit period is from 1 April to 31 March the following year.

Public Holidays — You are entitled to 8 days public holidays. Entitlement to, and payment for, public holidays shall be in accordance with Working Rule 19.

9   Sick Pay – in addition to SSP your entitlement to sick pay is in accordance with Working Rule 20.

10   Pension and Benefits Scheme – You are entitled to payments in accordance with the Building and Civil Engineering Benefits Scheme. Details of which are available from ....or from B&CE Holidays Scheme Management Ltd, Manor Royal, Crawley, West Sussex RH10 2QP.

11   Length of Notice of Termination to be given: Working Rule 24
By Employer:
Less than 4 weeks service – 1 day
4 weeks but less than 2 years service – 1 week
2 years service or more – 1 week for each completed year of service to a maximum of 12 weeks after 12 years
By employee:
Less than 4 weeks – 1 day
4 weeks service or more – 1 week

12   Any changes of the terms of employment will be notified to you within one month.
13   Employees must comply with the Company Safety Policy. Copies are available from ....
14   I accept the above statement of particulars of terms of employment.

Signed ....   Date.......................

NOTE
1   DISCIPLINARY RULES are laid down in Working Rule 23.
2   GRIEVANCES, DISPUTES AND DIFFERENCES
A grievance arising from any disciplinary decision concerning your employment should in the first instance be raised verbally with your immediate supervisor.
Steps for dealing with issues or grievances you may have arising from or relating to the employment to which this statement relates should, in the first instance be raised verbally with your immediate supervisor. If the grievance is unresolved you may use the procedure set out in Working Rule 22.
3   CONTRACTING OUT CERTIFICATE
Contracting out certificate arrangements do not apply to your contract of employment.

Fig. 1.   *Written statement of employment suggested by the Construction Industry Joint Council (copied with the kind permission of the Construction Industry Joint Council)*

other industrial action are prohibited until such times as the parties to the dispute have sought resolution through the conciliation procedure.

An interesting development in relation to the CIJC Working Rule Agreement is the emergence of 'Template' from the Building and Civil Engineering (B&CE) Annual Holidays and Benefit Schemes.[4] The Template scheme has come about as a direct result of the changes that were needed in the B&CE holiday pay scheme following the introduction of the Working Time Regulations 1998.

See Fig. 1 for a written statement of employment suggested by the CIJC.

3.3. NATIONAL AGREEMENT FOR THE ENGINEERING CONSTRUCTION INDUSTRY

The National Agreement for the Engineering Construction Industry (NAECI) first came into force in November 1981 to exert discipline over the engineering construction industry which in the 1960s and 1970s was characterised in the words of a National Economic Development Office report 'on all major contracts being late and overspent, and by the existence of a highly unstable industrial relations climate'. Industrial disputes were commonplace because the agreements which preceded the NAECI were imprecise and left too many significant terms and conditions of employment to be negotiated at site level.

By the second half of the 1970s, a consensus had built up within the industry that there was an urgent need for change. Negotiations began which concluded in the creation of the NAECI and the National Joint Council for the Engineering Construction Industry in 1981. The implementation of the NAECI has led to a significant reduction in industrial disputes and an improvement in industrial relations.

The National Agreement for the Engineering Construction Industry is negotiated between

- Employers' representatives
  - Engineering Construction Industry Association
  - Thermal Insulation Contractors Association
  - Electrical Contractors Association of Scotland
- Trade unions
  - Amalgamated Engineering & Electrical Union (AEEU)
  - GMB
  - TGWU
  - Manufacturing, Science and Finance Union (MSF)

The NAECI was concluded on 10 September and was revised on 16 December 1998. It is stated to apply to all employees who are hourly paid within the industry. The scope of the industry is defined by setting out the types of work that are taken to be part of the industry.[5] The NAECI also makes it clear that employment in the industry is conditional upon the parties agreeing to the NAECI and confirms that the agreement forms part of the employee's contract of employment.

The objectives of the NAECI are as follows

- To improve and maintain the cost effectiveness of the Engineering Construction Industry to make its performance competitive.
- To encourage the Industry's expansion and to create more business opportunities with greater stability of employment.
- To provide earnings for the workforce which reflect the achievement of higher productivity.

The NAECI is characterised by its detailed drafting; relatively high basic rates of pay; a strict control over the extent of local agreement over wages and bonus earnings or second tier payments; the restriction of excessive overtime working, and the encouragement of progressive shift arrangements. The NAECI's detailed drafting is indicative of its intention to limit the scope for local bargaining and therefore the potential for disputes.

A particular feature of the NAECI is the ability of the National Joint Council to 'nominate' major projects which are of sufficient size and significance to the construction industry as a whole for the National Joint Council to be concerned to monitor their progress closely. Nomination is stated to assist in the 'objective of bringing stability to industrial relations with an associated improvement in productivity'.[6] On a nominated project, on-site industrial relations are managed by both the contractors and the unions. Once nominated, projects are preceded by a 'pre-job conference' at which the client, the unions and contractors discuss the project programme, its duration, the anticipated manning levels and the methods of working. From this pre-job conference, a Project Joint Council (PJC) is established to oversee industrial relations for the duration of the project. The PJC is constituted from the principal contractors, the local union's full-time officers and a shop steward from each section of each union. It meets monthly. The NAECI provides detailed rules as to its constitution, rules and jurisdiction. It receives reports on site progress and an audit report on the payroll of each contractor. This audit report highlights any deviation from the payments that are to be properly paid under the NAECI. The employers' ability to make payments at their discretion and the unions' freedom to demand higher wages are thus circumscribed.

In order to co-ordinate the industrial relations policies of the various contractors on a Nominated Project, the PJC negotiates a Supplementary Project Agreement which covers all the items which the NAECI allows to be locally agreed at site level (within the strict parameters set by the NAECI), which include

- hours of work
- breaks
- overtime arrangements
- the bonus scheme to be applied
- when fixed holidays will be taken
- the issue of protective clothing
- site security
- parking arrangements.

When the Nominated Project nears completion, the PJC meet to discuss de-nomination, future programming and commissioning of the works. At a time after completion of the works, the PJC will again meet with the client and the principal participants at a post-job conference to analyse job records and learn lessons for the future.

The NAECI provides that derogations allowed under the Working Time Regulations 1998 should apply. For instance, the reference period to measure the 48-hour week minimum has been extended from 17 to 52 weeks. Furthermore, the rest provisions set out in the NAECI expressly supersede the weekly, daily and rest breaks provided for in the Working Time Regulations 1998.

3.4. The National Industry Rules of the Joint Industry Board for the Electrical Contracting Industry

The National Working Rules of the Joint Industry Board for the Electrical Contracting Industry (JIB Agreement) are stated to apply to all 'operatives engaged in electrical contracting' in England and Wales. Electricians in Scotland have a separate agreement with the Scottish electrical contractors. The two agreements have been entirely separate in the past, but the principal items are now gradually being harmonised.

The JIB Agreement first came into being in 1968 following a series of strikes and lockouts in the 1950s and early 1960s which had given electrical contracting a poor reputation. The industrial relations between the unions and the employers' association were poor. The old Industrial Agreement allowed a wide variety of plus payments for abnormal conditions and these were used as devices to claim increases in pay at site level and were frequently used for political purposes to stop production and construction. The unions, the employers' association and their respective members feared that unless the situation was brought under control, the industry would suffer permanent damage and lose its highly-trained workforce. After a new executive was elected at the AEEU, the AEEU and the employers' association embarked on a policy of negotiating long-term agreements to avoid the annual wage confrontation, which had been the norm in the past. The new agreement, which was signed in 1968, bought out all the locally agreed site payments and has succeeded in bringing stability to the industry.

The 1968 JIB Agreement, as well as providing for annual wage increases, also provided for the setting up of the Joint Industry Board (JIB) to replace the existing National and Area Joint Industrial Councils.

The JIB Agreement is negotiated between

- Employers' representative
  - ○ Electrical Contractors' Association

- Trade union
  - ○ AEEU (Electrical, Electronic, Telecommunications and Plumbing Union (EETPU) section).

The objects of the JIB are as follows

To regulate the relations between employers and employees engaged in the Industry and to provide all kinds of benefits for persons concerned with the Industry in such ways as the Joint Industry Board may think fit, for the purpose of stimulating and furthering the improvement and progress of the Industry for the mutual advantage of the employers and employees engaged therein, and, in particular, for the purpose aforesaid and in the public interest, to regulate and control employment and productive capacity within the Industry and the level of skill and proficiency, wages and welfare benefits of persons concerned in the Industry.

The aim of the JIB Agreement is akin to the NAECI: the parties to the JIB Agreement seek at all times to develop a common approach to all the problems which are encountered by the industry not only in their own interests but in the public interest.

Today, the JIB is governed by its National Board which consists of 15 representatives from the AEEU, 15 representatives from the Electrical Contractors' Association and Public Interest member(s). It meets under its independent chairman, currently Sir Michael Latham. Sir Michael Latham is required not only to chair meetings at the JIB but also to ensure that, in its discussions, the JIB maintains its high principles of mutual co-operation and that the public interest is also taken into account.

In addition there is a system of Regional Joint Industry Boards. The country is divided into 13 regions. Each regional board has a chairman and deputy chairman and up to 16 members, all of whom are appointed by the National Board. Regional Boards are comprised of eight employers' representatives and eight union representatives. The regional boards are responsible for everything which occurs within their region and can decide all disputes affecting the employment of labour within the JIB Agreement (although only the JIB can decide wages and conditions of employment).

The JIB Agreement, like the NAECI, sets relatively high national wage rates and there is virtually no scope for negotiation at site level. Overtime is discouraged by the JIB Agreement. The permission of the regional boards is required if systematic overtime in excess of the 37½-hour normal working week is worked. The JIB Agreement relies on a clearly defined grading structure, from technicians to labourers to electricians.

On major projects, both nominated and non-nominated under the NAECI, the JIB has recognised the need to harmonise the earnings potential of craftsmen employed under the NAECI and JIB Agreement. As a consequence the JIB Agreement sets a second tier productivity payment for nominated projects and permits overtime in line with the hours agreed in any Supplementary Project Agreement agreed under the NAECI.

There are provisions in the JIB Agreement for Controlled Financial Incentive Schemes, but the use of such formal schemes tends to be limited. However, electrical contractors and their employees frequently organise more informal bonus arrangements. These do not tend to cause problems on minor projects but would not be tolerated on major projects particularly those which are nominated under NAECI.

As with NAECI, the JIB Agreement uses the derogations allowed under the Working Time Regulations 1998 and extends the reference period over which the 48-hour working week

ELECTRICAL OPERATIVES (Including Apprentices) employed under JIB Terms and Conditions – the constituent parties to the JIB are the Electrical Contractors Association and the AEEU.

STATEMENT

of particulars of terms of employment pursuant to

THE EMPLOYMENT PROTECTION (CONSOLIDATION) ACT 1978

as amended by the **Trade Union Reform and Employment Rights Act, 1993**

and the

CONTRACTS OF EMPLOYMENT AND REDUNDANCY PAYMENTS ACT (NORTHERN IRELAND) 1965

Amended by Industrial Relations (N.I.) Order 1976

Please type or use capitals with ball point pen – make sure **all** copies are clear

1.   Name of employer ....

     Address   From: ....

2.   To: Name of Employee .... (Surname) .... (Full Christian Name)

       Address .... (Number/Name of House) .... (Street or Road)

       .... (Town) .... (County) .... (Post Code)

       National Insurance No .... Works No ..../None*

3.   Date of commencement of Employment .... / .... / ....

                                                           (Day)   (Month)   (Year)

A previous Employer is associated company or some company under new ownership the date on which the continuous period of employment began should be stated.)

4.   **Date of this Statement** ....

                                          (Day)   (Month)   (Year)

5.   (i)   Position .... (insert JIB Grading) ..../Apprentice*

     1   Current Rate of Pay. £ ....

     2   Hours of Work ....

     3   Pay Period; *weekly/month

     4   Holiday entitlement:

         Annual Holidays ....

     3.   Public Holidays ....

     5   You have been:

    (ii)   *Shop Recruited in which capacity you are liable to be transferred to work on any site on which your Employer has a contract. Location of shop if different from 1. above:

       ....

    (iii)   *Locally Engaged in accordance with National Working Rule 12(f). Site initially engaged.

         (i)   Further details of your rate of wages pay period, hours of work, conditions relating to holidays, public holidays and holiday pay and terms and conditions relating to your incapacity for work due to sickness or injury and sick pay are in accordance with the provisions of the following documents:

            (a)   your pay slip or pay envelope;

44

(b) the current JIB Handbook incorporating the National Working Rules and the Industrial Determinations as determined by the Joint Industry Board for the Electrical Contracting Industry as applicable to the shop or site where you are for the time being employed and the JIB Benefits Scheme;

(c) the incentive scheme, if any, applying to your work or job;

(d) *the Joint Industry Board's Training Schemes;

(e) *the Standard Training Contract issued by the Joint Industry Board.

(ii) You are entitled to receive, and obliged to give, notice of termination of employment in accordance with the provisions of the Employment Protection (Consolidation) Act 1978, in Northern Ireland the Contracts of Employment and Redundancy Payments Act (Northern Ireland), 1965, as amended, and the National Working Rules and Industrial Determinations referred to in paragraphs 6(b) above.

(iii) You will automatically become a member of the JIB Pension Scheme ("the Scheme") [details of which have been given to you] unless you expressly opt out by notice in writing, to your Employer (which you may give at any time). For the purpose of the foregoing, signing and returning a copy of this statement to your Employer constitutes (i) an application for admission to the Scheme and (ii) authority to your Employer to make the appropriate deductions, (having regard to the amount of your pay) from your pay in respect of your contributions to the Scheme.

Retirement takes place at normal retirement age for the Company.

(iv) A contracting-out certificate is/is not* in force in respect of your employment and the State Pension Scheme.

(v) Your employment is conditional upon you abiding by the National Working Rules and Industrial Determinations for the Electrical Contracting Industry the Disputes Procedure set out in Section 3 of the current JIB Handbook and the following safety and disciplinary rules of your employer ....(to be specified)

(vi) Any grievance you may have arising from or relating to the employment to which this statement relates or any dissatisfaction with any disciplinary decision relating to you should in the first instance be raised with your immediate supervisor. If your grievance or dissatisfaction remains unresolved and it is no longer possible for you to appeal to a more senior member of the management the subsequent steps in the procedure are as prescribed in the Disputes Procedure referred to in paragraph 10 above.

(vii) Copies of the documents referred to in this statement will be made available for inspection by you during the course of your employment upon request and any future changes in the terms of employment will be entered up on these documents, or otherwise recorded for reference, within one month of the change.

(viii) To be completed only in respect of Apprentices or Electrical Operatives with a fixed-term contract of employment for more than 4 weeks:

The date of termination of your period of Apprenticeship*/the Deed of Apprenticeship*/or fixed-term contract of employment* is ....

I agree that the terms and conditions set out above (a copy of which I have received) and the terms and conditions contained in the documents referred to above (as varied from time to time) are the principal terms and conditions of my employment.

Signed ....

Delete if not applicable   See Notes Overleaf

Fig. 2. *Written statement of employment suggested by the Joint Industry Board of the Electrical Contracting Industry (reproduced with kind permission of the Joint Industry Board of the Electrical Contracting Industry)*

maximum is to be measured from 17 to 52 weeks. It also supersedes the provisions for weekly, daily and rest breaks contained in the Working Time Regulations 1998. The JIB has also produced an extended *Code of Practice* to govern certain aspects of the employment relationship including

- recruitment
- written statement of employment
- disciplinary procedures
- the use of subcontractors/self-employed (which is only permitted in certain circumstances).

The JIB Agreement also provides for a benefit credit allocation system called the JIB Annual Holiday with Pay Scheme which is operated by the Electrical Contracting Industry Benefits Agency.

Special provisions are also made for certain industries including

- shipping
- oil and gas — offshore
- cable work
- engineering construction sites.

See Fig. 2 for a written statement of employment suggested by the Joint Industry Board of the Electrical Contracting Industry.

3.5. The National Agreement as to Working Rules for Operatives in the Heating, Ventilating, Air Conditioning, Piping and Domestic Engineering Industry

The National Agreement as to Working Rules for Operatives in the Heating, Ventilating, Air Conditioning, Piping and Domestic Engineering Industry (HVAC Agreement) is negotiated between

- Employers' representative
  o Heating and Ventilating Contractors' Association (HVCA)

- Trade union
  - ᴐ MSF.

The HVAC Agreement was first issued in 1911 as a mechanism principally for establishing recognised pay rates for the trades then employed in the industry. The HVAC Agreement has developed and evolved over the years to set the basic terms and conditions of employment of operatives employed in the industry. As the name suggests, the scope of the HVAC Agreement comprises work related to the heating, ventilating, air conditioning, piping and domestic engineering industry. This includes

- all forms of piping, including gas installations and plastic pipework
- all forms of boilers, including oil-fired installations
- sprinkler (fire protection) installations
- heated ceilings, ductwork erection and thermal insulation
- associated service and maintenance.

The HVAC Agreement includes a well-defined graded pay structure which reflects working practices within the industry and the integral part played by welding in much of the industry's activities. The grades[7] are defined by a combination of factors relating either to competence and/or conditions agreed between the two sides of industry and overseen through the National Joint Industrial Council (NJIC). The NJIC is also responsible for overseeing the industry's apprentice training arrangements.

Pay for annual and public holidays, sick pay and certain other welfare benefits (such as death benefit) is provided by WELPLAN, the industry's welfare and holiday scheme administered by a wholly owned subsidiary company of HVCA, H&V Welfare Limited.

As with other agreements in the industry, the HVAC Agreement reflects the view that it is in the long-term interests of both sides of the industry to have a directly employed labour force. The NJIC considers that employers should not employ subcontractors who are not bona fide employers of labour observing the appropriate recognised wage rate and working conditions. The NJIC hopes that by drafting this policy into the HVAC Agreement, the industry will underpin the directly employed labour force and prevent the industry's training effort being jeopardised by the use of self-employed operatives. The HVAC Agreement also uses the derogations set out in the Working Time Regulations 1998 to exclude the regulatory obligations in relation to weekly rest, daily rest and rest breaks, preferring to rely on the rest periods provided in the HVAC Agreement. The reference period for measuring the 48-hour maximum working week has been changed from 17 to 52 weeks.

As for bonuses and allowances, the HVAC, in certain circumstances, allows for

- responsibility allowances
- merit money (where payment is made at the option of the employer for mobility, loyalty, long service and the like, and for special skill over and above the norm)
- target incentive schemes.

There is no industry-wide administrative apparatus for limiting or sanctioning overtime working but the HVAC Agreement recognises that overtime must be contained and provides that overtime should only be used in cases of emergency or urgency. Special terms and conditions are applicable where operatives are working on a 'nominated' engineering project as set out in Appendix C to the HVAC Agreement.

NOTES

1. as the CIJC Agreement and JIB Agreements provide
2. as it was then called, now the Construction Confederation
3. formerly the Building Employers' Confederation
4. which is discussed in greater detail in Chapter 5
5. Working Rule 3.2
6. Working Rule 10.1
7. which were revised in August 1998

Table 3. Schedule of the main industry terms of employment

	Construction Industry Joint Council Working Rule Agreement	National Agreement for the Engineering Construction Industry	National Working Rules of the Joint Industry Board for the Electrical Industry	Heating, Ventilating etc. National Agreement
1. Date of Agreement	29 June 1998	16 December 1998	30 March 1998	9 May 1999
2. Date of implementation of last wage increase	6 January 1997	4 January 1999	7 February 2000	23 August 1999
3. Date of next wage review	29 June 2000	To be arranged	8 January 2001	To be arranged
4. Rates of pay	Craft rate £6.05 Basic Skill Rate 4: £4.90 3: £5.20 2: £5.55 1: £5.76	Grade 6 £7.77 Grade 5: £7.40 Grade 4: £7.03 Grade 3: £5.92 (£4.44 for a 17 year old) Grade 2: £5.17 (£3.87 for a 17 year old and £3.10 for a 16 year old) Grade 5: £7.40 Grade 4: £7.03 Grade 3: £5.92 (£4.44 for a 17 year old) Grade 2: £5.17 (£3.87 for a 17 year old and £3.10 for a 16 year old)	All grades have varying hourly rates depending upon whether they are: • shop reporting; • job reporting (transport provided); or • job reporting (own transport) • Technician: £8.94 to £9.49 • Approved Electrician: £7.82 to £8.37 • Electrician: £7.13 to £7.68	Foreman: £8.73 Senior craftsman: £7.79 to £7.48 Craftsman: £6.86 Installer/Improver: £6.23 Assistant: £5.82 Adult Trainee: £5.25

Table 3 (continued)

	Construction Industry Joint Council Working Rule Agreement	National Agreement for the Engineering Construction Industry	National Working Rules of the Joint Industry Board for the Electrical Industry	Heating, Ventilating etc. National Agreement
	Basic Unskilled Labour Rate £4.55	Grade 1: Adult £4.44 17 year old: £3.33 16 year old: £2.66	Labourer: £5.52 to £6.07	Mate over 18: £5.25 Junior Mate 17-18: £3.37 Junior Mate to 17: £2.43
	Skilled Operative Additional Rate III: £0.20 II: £0.70 I: £1.15	N/A	N/A However, responsibility money is paid between 10p and £1.00 per hour (as agreed locally) to supervisors.	N/A Responsibility allowance: Craftsman and Senior Craftsman: 31p/62p
5. Productivity bonus schemes and fixed rate bonus payments	As agreed locally	Second tier payments available at varying levels depending on the circumstances, which may include: • Incentive bonus scheme; • In lieu payment; and • Productivity allowance.	No rules in agreement Profit Related Pay allowed (subject to conditions)	Merit money can be agreed locally for mobility, loyalty, long service, or special skill. Target incentive schemes are allowed – to be agreed locally

6.	Temporary lay-off	May be agreed as an alternative to redundancy.	May be agreed as an alternative to redundancy.	Conditional upon: 1 every reasonable effort to attend site; 2 employer shall make representations to the client to gain access; 3 AEEU shall be informed and shall make its best endeavours to gain access; 4 operatives should then be redeployed.	May be mutually agreed in the event of industrial dislocation
7.	Guaranteed minimum payment per week	Payment for the first 5 days of temporary lay-off in any three month period. Guarantee is lost in event of break in continuity of work due to industrial action on site, Tide Work or work paid by shift	For employees employed for not less than 4 weeks, payment up to 38 hours at their basic rate for the whole or part of the pay week. Guarantee is lost if production on site is disrupted or industrial dispute has affected work and the employee has received one week's payment.	Statutory guarantee payment. Payment for 5 days in any three month period.	For operatives with at least 2 weeks' service 38 hours in any normal week at basic rate. Guarantee is lost if dislocation of production is caused by industrial action.
8.	Inclement weather provisions	Temporary lay-off provisions apply	Normal rate plus enhancements for those who have returned to temporary shelters. Otherwise, basic rate.	Guaranteed minimum applies	Guaranteed minimum applies

	Construction Industry Joint Council Working Rule Agreement	National Agreement for the Engineering Construction Industry	National Working Rules of the Joint Industry Board for the Electrical Industry	Heating, Ventilating etc. National Agreement
9. Lodging/ subsistence allowance	£21.09 per night Where the operative is necessarily living away from the place he normally resides	Daily rate: £18.35 Weekly rate: £128.45 Special rates apply to public holiday, annual holiday, sickness and inner London.	£22.40 per night	£22.75 per night
10. Daily travel allowance	£3.49 to £15.56 For travel between 15 and 75 kilometres measured one way from home to job/site. Fraction of kilometres to be rounded up	Two Scales for distances over two miles to over 35 miles: Scale 1: for those employees who travel by their own means Scale 2: where suitable free transport is available. Scale 1: £3.57 to £16.28 Scale 2: £2.43 to £10.92	Under 10 miles: Nil 10–15 miles: £2.13 + £4.26 15–20 miles: £3.82 + £5.10 20–25 miles: £4.61 + £5.95 25–30 miles: £5.56 + £6.85 30–55 miles: £8.25 + £8.25 55–75 miles: £9.70 + £9.70 (for each additional 75 miles, £2.50)	Rates are split between craftsman and assistants; mates and trainees 10–20 miles: £3.49 - £3.30 20–30 miles: £6.26 - £5.40 30–40 miles: £8.24 - £7.10 40–50 miles: £10.28 - £8.81
11. Protective clothing, tool payments, etc.	None provided	2 Boiler suits and pair of safety boots every 12 months	Safety Helmets: locally agreed. Protective clothing required by law: provided free of charge.	Safety helmets and boots to be supplied. Operatives to supply rules and spirit level.

No.		Column 1	Column 2	Column 3	Column 4
12.	Abnormal conditions	Stone cleaning: 0.45 per hour Tunnels: 0.12 per hour Sewer Works: 0.20-0.30 per hour	Tunnels: 5-8 ft: 3.5p 3-5ft: 5p Under 3 ft: 9p Welders: 8p to 25p	N/A	£2.99 per day.
13.	Height money (dependent on height work takes place)	0.25 per hour	50-75 ft: 2p 75-100 ft: 4p 100-150 ft: 6p 150-200 ft: 11p 200-250 ft: 16p 250-300 ft: 21p and 5p for additional 50 ft	N/A	N/A
14.	Normal working week	39 hours. Monday to Thursday: 8 hours per day Friday: 7 hours	38 hours. Monday to Thursday: 8 hours per day Friday: 6 hours	37½ hours day workers 7½ hours per day 38 hours shift workers	38 hours
15.	Shift and night working	All of the Agreements make provision for shift and night working, for which there are additional payments			
16.	Entitlement to paid annual holidays in a full year	21 days '7 at Christmas, 4 at Easter and 10 in the Summer' Template' Scheme applies.	25 days (min of 5 at Christmas, 5 at another existing annual or public holiday and 15 by agreement)	As determined by the JIB Annual Holiday with Pay Scheme from time to time (currently 7 days Winter, 4 days Spring and 11 days Summer)	23 days (4 Spring holidays' 12 Summer holidays; and 7 Winter holidays) WELPLAN Scheme applies
17.	Number of days of statutory holiday entitlement per annum	8 days	8 days	8 days	8 days

Table 3 (continued)

	Construction Industry Joint Council Working Rule Agreement	National Agreement for the Engineering Construction Industry	National Working Rules of the Joint Industry Board for the Electrical Industry	Heating, Ventilating etc. National Agreement
18. Weekday overtime payment	Cannot be unreasonably refused @1½ basic for the first four hours, then double time.	Regular overtime is 'not in the industry's interests' NJC approval may be required @1½ basic – after midnight: double time	Deprecated by JIB. However, Regional JIB may allow overtime in certain circumstances. Overtime payments only became due after 38 hours have been worked. After 7pm or before 7am @ 1½ basic. 15% uplift for flexible workers, and overtime after 38 hours.	Time worked over 38 hours per week @ 1½ basic. Hours over 12 hours in a day, double time.
19. Saturday overtime payment	Cannot be unreasonably refused @1½ basic for the first four hours, then double time.	@1½ basic for the first four hours before noon, then double time	@ 1½ basic until 1pm, thereafter, double time	@ 1½ basic (for first 5 hours) – thereafter, double time
20. Sunday overtime payment	Double time	Double time	Double time N.B. special call-out rates also apply	Double time

21.	Sickness benefit (paid in addition to Statutory Sick Pay)	A maximum of 50 days pay (excluding the first three days)	CIGNA Scheme. Weekly benefit of £40.00 excluding the first three days' absence up to 52 weeks	Industry sick pay scheme: after 14 weeks service, up to 26 weeks benefit in any 52 weeks period @ £65.00 per week.	Up to 52 weeks. For first 28 weeks, from £4.90 per week to £179.13 per week. For weeks 29 to 52, from £35.77 to £86.90 per week (depending upon the Credit Value Category for each grade).
22.	Death and accidental injury	In accordance with the Building and Civil Engineering Benefits Scheme	CIGNA Scheme £20 000 permanent total disablement, £32 000 total benefit of Occupational Fatal Accident	JIB Insurance, Accidental Death, Dismemberment and Permanent and Total Disability schemes: £15 000 permanent total disability benefit; £17 000 Death benefits.	WELPLAN Scheme £38 600 Death benefit; £17 000 accidental dismemberment; Up to £17 000 permanent total disability benefit
23.	Notice of termination of employment	By employee: Up to 4 weeks: 1 day After 4 weeks: 1 week By employer: First 4 weeks: 1 day 4 weeks to 2 years: 1 week 2 years to 12 years: 1 week for each full year 12 years or over: 12 weeks	By employee: After 4 weeks: 1 week By employer: 4 weeks to 2 years: 1 week: After 2 years: 2 weeks; 2 years to 12 years: 1 week for each full year of employment up to 12 years or over: 12 weeks Severance pay up to 103 weeks at between £4.23 and £2.60 per week employed up to 2 years (when statutory redundancy pay applies)	By employee: Up to 4 weeks: 1 day After 4 weeks: 1 week By employer: Up to 4 weeks: 1 day 4 weeks to 2 years: 1 week 2 weeks to 12 years: 1 week for each full year Over 12 years: 12 weeks (statutory redundancy pay with right to paid time off to look for work and discussions with AEEU)	By operative: Up to 5 days: remainder of working day (more than 2 hours) 5 days–4 weeks: remainder of working week (more than 1 day) More than 4 weeks: 1 week By employer: Up to 5 days: remainder of working day (more than 2 hours) 5 days–4 weeks: remainder of working week (more than 1 day) 4 weeks–2 years: 1 week

Table 3 (continued)

	Construction Industry Joint Council Working Rule Agreement	National Agreement for the Engineering Construction Industry	National Working Rules of the Joint Industry Board for the Electrical Industry	Heating, Ventilating etc. National Agreement
				2 years–12 years: 1 week for each full year of employment up to 12 weeks.
24	Pension arrangements within collective agreements	In accordance with the Building and Civil Engineering Benefits Scheme	Engineering Construction Workers Pension Scheme (run by Scottish Widows)	No rules in agreement	H & V Pensions available Voluntary Scheme

4

PAYE/NIC — the clamp-down

As a large number of employment-related rights apply only to a worker who is able to show that he is an employee,[1] the determination of a worker's status will have a substantial impact on the extent of the legal protection to which he is entitled. The employment status of a worker also impacts upon their tax position, determining the method by which the Inland Revenue will collect income tax and the appropriate class of National Insurance contributions (NICs) payable. An employee will have a payment on account of his Schedule E income tax liability withheld at source by his employer through the PAYE scheme and will also have employees' Class 1 NICs deducted at source. His employer will be liable to pay employers' NICs. However, the self-employed subcontractor will pay Class 2 and possibly Class 4 NICs, depending on his profits, while his employer will pay no employers' NICs. The self-employed subcontractor will have his income tax collected following the end of the tax year through the self-assessment scheme.[2]

As early as the late 1960s the Inland Revenue recognised that a number of workers who had been treated as self-employed subcontractors in the construction industry were avoiding the

57

payment of income tax and NICs. While employees would pay Schedule E income tax and Class 1 NICs at source through PAYE, significant numbers of workers claiming self-employment could not be relied upon to account properly for income tax and Class 2 or Class 4 NICs at the end of each tax year. In order to ensure that tax was collected from these subcontractors on 'the lump', in 1972 the Inland Revenue introduced the Construction Industry Tax Deduction Scheme, with its accompanying 714 certificates and SC60 tax vouchers (the 714 Scheme). As such, any subcontractor in the construction industry who attended site with a valid 714 certificate (which was issued by the Inland Revenue) could be paid gross of income tax. Otherwise, the subcontractors would have lower rate income tax deducted at source through the SC60 voucher scheme. In both cases, the final tax assessment was calculated and accounted for at the end of the tax year by means of the subcontractor's tax return. The system allowed the Inland Revenue to collect income tax at source from a large number of subcontractors who had not been able to obtain a 714 certificate.

To be entitled to be paid gross, construction subcontractors had to satisfy the Inland Revenue that they were entitled to 714 certificates. Qualification for a 714 certificate depended on the subcontractor

(a) being a subcontractor in the UK
(b) being employed or self-employed in the UK for a continuous period of three years in the six years before applying for the 714 certificate
(c) having paid all income tax and NIC due for a continuous period of three years in the six years before applying for the 714 certificate
(d) running his business properly with proper stock, from proper premises and with proper records.

For those who did not qualify for a 714 certificate, but maintained that they were self-employed, they were paid through the SC60 tax deduction voucher scheme. Their employer was obliged to deduct lower rate income tax at source and remit a voucher evidencing such a deduction to the Inland Revenue. The employer provided the subcontractor with a form SC60 as evidence of the deduction. More recently, the Inland Revenue came to the view that the 714 Scheme was being abused. While acknowledging that the Inland Revenue had itself turned a blind eye to the abuse to some extent, it took the view that a large number of workers who were holding themselves out as subcontractors (either with 714 certificates or as SC60 voucher holders) would be more accurately categorised as employees. Frequently, the Inland Revenue discovered workers classified and paid as employees working on the same contracts, under the same terms of engagement, in the same way and on the same construction site as 714 or SC60 subcontractors, while the two sets of workers were being taxed in different ways.

As a result, the Inland Revenue decided to review the taxation of construction workers in two significant ways

- It introduced measures which sought to force construction companies to change the manner by which they classified their workers.
- It replaced the 714 Scheme with the Construction Industry Scheme (CIS).

These changes were designed to recover an extra £100 million in unpaid tax and NICs from the industry and are commonly referred to as the Inland Revenue 'clamp-down'.

4.2. CLASSIFICATION OF WORKERS

In 1995, the Inland Revenue put the construction industry on notice that from 5 April 1996[3] the issuing of a 714 certificate by the Inland Revenue to a worker in the industry would not necessarily mean that that worker was a subcontractor in the Inland Revenue's eyes. The 714 certificate could no longer be treated as conclusive of a subcontractor's status. The Inland Revenue made it clear that the burden lay on employers in the industry to make sure that they had classified their workers correctly, whether they were 714 certificate or SC60 voucher holders. Employers were reminded that proper collection of income tax and NICs was down to them. While this first stage of the Inland Revenue's clamp-down was recognised as introducing a fundamental change in the manner in which the industry engaged its workforce in that some workers were pushed towards employee status, there was no change in the law involved; the clamp-down merely introduced a change in the Inland Revenue's practice in enforcing the law.

To persuade the industry that this first stage of the clamp-down should be taken seriously, the Inland Revenue made it clear that it could seek from the employer repayment of all income tax for which the worker had failed to account in the event of deliberate avoidance or fraud by an employer. Alternatively, the Inland Revenue indicated that it would seek repayment of income tax back to at least the implementation date of the clamp-down[4] if an inspector found that an employer had incorrectly, albeit unintentionally, classified its workforce. Employers were faced with the possibility of substantial historic income tax and NIC liabilities as well as an increase in future labour overhead costs. Recognising that the new arrangements would have a significant impact on construction companies, both in terms of the potential increase in companies' labour costs and in terms of the difficulties in achieving an accurate classification,[5] the Inland Revenue and the then Contributions Agency issued leaflets[6] explaining to employers and to workers in the industry how, in the Inland Revenue's opinion, employment and subcontractor status could be distinguished. These factors have been listed in Section 2.3.

Following representations from the industry, the Inland Revenue recognised that despite the guidance given in the leaflets, even the most reputable company could face a claim for substantial arrears of income tax and NICs, referable back to the clamp-down's implementation date.[7] Notwithstanding the company's best efforts in reclassifying its workforce properly, this liability could arise merely by reason of the fact that an inspector disagreed with the employer's determination of the status of the workers. The Inland Revenue acknowledged the difficulties associated with achieving a correct determination of employment status. As a result, the Inland Revenue intimated that if, following an inspection by the Inland Revenue, companies were found to have made a bona fide attempt at the reclassification of their workers and took relevant workers onto their books as employees (where appropriate) the Inland Revenue would not seek to reclaim historic income tax and NICs, but would only enforce the reclassification (and the repayment of income tax and NICs) from the date of the Inland Revenue inspection. However, despite this indication from the Inland Revenue it has been reported in the construction press that following Inland Revenue inspections, some companies have been required to settle claims for arrears of tax and NICs back to 6 April 1997, despite making bona fide attempts at reclassification.

4.2.1. Practical steps to aid classification

The greater the certainty which can be achieved by employers in determining their workers' status to the Inland Revenue's satisfaction the better. In that respect, and in conjunction with the guidance set out in Chapter 2, the following steps might usefully be considered:

Keep records and notes of action taken
As the Inland Revenue has stated that it will not seek to recover backdated tax beyond the date of inspection where a bona fide attempt at reclassification has been made, employers should be *seen* to have reacted properly to the Inland Revenue's clamp-down policy. To evidence this, and in preparation for an inspection, employers should keep all records and notes of all meetings and advice received in relation to the issue. All papers should be kept in one place so that they are easily obtainable in the event of an inspection. File notes should record the decisions made and the basis of those decisions.

Reference to the Inland Revenue leaflets

Employers' decisions, in so far as it is possible, should refer to the Inland Revenue's explanatory leaflets.[8] These leaflets contain the particular factors which the Inland Revenue has confirmed it will take into account in judging the status of a worker. The more that an employer can be seen to have adhered to those factors, the easier it will be to persuade an Inspector that the employer's classification is correct.

Consider obtaining prior approval

Where an employer is unsure as to the status of a worker, or a group of workers, the Inland Revenue can be approached for a determination. Even though the approach may be made anonymously through the employer's solicitor or accountant, some companies nevertheless may be cautious about such action, due to the employer's fear that in explaining the background to the relevant workers' engagement, the employer's anonymity may be lost. It would also be reasonable to anticipate that the Inland Revenue would lean towards a finding of employment status in its determination.

Time/site records

Each employer should keep time/site records of

- how its workforce has been engaged
- the length of its workers' engagement
- the terms under which they were engaged
- the manner in which they worked.

Without these records, it will be difficult for employers to satisfy an Inspector that they have properly classified their workers.

Draft subcontractor/employee contracts

Employers should consider highlighting the differences between their employees and their subcontractors in the drafting of their employee and subcontractor contracts. In this way, the justification for an employer's classification can be made easier. These contracts should, where possible, include express reference to those factors which the Inland Revenue considers determinative as to status. These include terms dealing with

- method of payment and invoicing
- tendering
- control
- the right to use a substitute or helper to do the job
- financial risk
- right of dismissal
- part and parcel of the organisation
- length of engagement
- whether the work is piecemeal
- whether the worker is entitled to sick and holiday pay
- supply of tools
- declaration of intention of the parties.

Changes in working practices
Generally, the issue of status is determined not only by a consideration of the contract terms but also by considering how the worker is engaged in practice. By showing a distinction between the treatment on site of subcontractors and employees, an employer is more likely to be able to justify his classification.

4.3. INSPECTION METHODS AND ENFORCEMENT

Since the start of the clamp-down in April 1997, there have been a number of methods used by the Inland Revenue to check employers' classifications of the status of their workers. In 1997, under the Conservative Government, Kenneth Clark introduced the 'Spend to Save' policy, whereby central funds were provided to the Inland Revenue to increase its inspection and enforcement capabilities. Greater numbers of inspectors were recruited by the Inland Revenue. In 1998, the Inland Revenue stated that 1200 site visits were completed — an increase in 28% from the previous year. Despite the increase in resources, the Inland Revenue estimated that it would take at least two years to inspect all construction companies. In the main, inspections relating to classification have occurred in the normal course of Inland Revenue site visits rather than through specific visitations, although site raids have occurred in some instances. The Inland Revenue has also stated that it will consider any complaints received that any companies are not abiding by the rules.

Despite the fact that the clamp-down has been in place for over three years, considerable confusion remains. The enforcement measures were designed to produce a level playing field, thereby not advantaging or disadvantaging any particular construction company as compared with another. However, due to the sporadic nature of inspections, together with different approaches adopted by individual inspectors in the various local tax offices, a level playing field has not been achieved. Construction companies, particularly smaller subcontractors, cannot be certain that companies with which they are competing have properly complied with the clamp-down. It can also be argued[9] that the factors to which the Inland Revenue has given particular weight when assessing status are not in line with the current legal position. It is arguable that the Inland Revenue's approach focuses too much upon whether or not a worker is in business on his own account. When their approach is considered against the background of the decisions of the courts on this point, it neither properly applies the multiple test nor gives the appropriate credit to the parties' intentions and the terms of the contract.[10]

4.4. Suggested schemes to avoid burdens

The increased overhead cost in taking large numbers of employees on to their books and paying employers' NICs has been a major concern for contractors. A number of schemes have been suggested as ways by which employers may be able to limit the effect of the clamp-down. Three schemes have emerged, each with its own advantages and disadvantages.

- agencies
- personal service companies
- partnerships.

An underlying issue for any employer considering these schemes is whether the chosen scheme will be seen by the Inland Revenue as having been established merely as a tax evasion mechanism, and will be ineffective as a consequence. Whatever the scheme, employers must remain aware of the Inland Revenue's power[11] to look to the objectives behind a legal structure to establish whether the scheme is set up for legitimate commercial reasons or whether it has been set up with the sole purpose of evading NICs and income tax which otherwise would be payable. However ingenious a scheme, it is always likely to be vulnerable to attack by the Inland Revenue on these grounds.

4.4.1. Agencies

Two types of agencies have been used by construction companies which are similar but subtly different: they are in-house agency companies engaging staff on a self-employed basis and external agency companies.

In-house agency companies
Under this scheme, workers who previously worked for a construction company are engaged as self-employed contractors through an agency company. The agency then supplies the workers

back to the construction company. Effectively the agency operates as a payroll provider; there is no direct contractual link between the workers and the construction company. As the agency pays the workers, the construction company is able to avoid NIC and PAYE payments. The scheme is of limited merit because the construction company will nevertheless have to fund the agency company, so the burden of tax and NICs will still be borne, albeit indirectly. Moreover, the advantage of avoiding the payment of PAYE seems now to have been lost following a change in the law[12] whereby agency workers must be paid by the agency by way of the PAYE scheme. Furthermore, the hope that NIC payments could be avoided seems also to have been dashed as the Inland Revenue now consider that workers engaged through an agency must pay NICs.[13] While employing workers through an agency can have its advantages, it no longer appears to be a way in which the effects of the clamp-down can be avoided. If the responsibility for payment of NIC and PAYE and any employment related liabilities are transferred to the agency, the fact that the construction company ultimately controls the agency means that the liabilities associated with the clamp-down are merely transferred within the group. Even if the transfer of these liabilities is in itself advantageous, NIC and PAYE payments must still be made.

External agency companies
A variant on the use of in-house agency companies involves sourcing labour through a company which is independent and which trades at arm's length with the construction company. An external agency company takes over the construction company's workforce and supplies labour as a subcontractor. The workforce perceives little difference in that it continues to work for the construction company. The advantage for the construction company is that the agency takes over the responsibility for

- proving that the workers are subcontractors
- any associated employment liabilities
- payment of NIC and PAYE.

Unlike the in-house agency type of scheme, these liabilities are passed to a third party. Unfortunately, however, the construction company loses control over its workforce. Moreover, the NIC and PAYE costs and any additional administration costs will be recharged to it from the agency company.

The extent to which this type of scheme will be effective in making a worker an employee of the agency rather than the construction company has been brought into question by a number of cases which have suggested that agency workers cannot be employees of labour agencies. For example in *Knights* v. *Anglican Industrial Services*, although a worker had been attached to an agency for three years, which had deducted PAYE and NICs, he was still held not to be an employee of the agency. However, in *McMeechan* v. *Secretary of State for Employment*, the Court of Appeal held that a temporary worker on the books of an employment agency may have had the status of an employee of that agency in respect of each assignment actually worked, notwithstanding the fact that the same worker may not have been entitled to employment status under his general terms of engagement with the agency. Furthermore, tribunals have recently questioned the historic presumption that an agency worker cannot be an employee of the construction company to which he is assigned.[14] Hence, one must query whether companies can remove completely the risks inherent in being found to be an agency employee's employer when the worker has been engaged through an agency.

For the reasons set out above, using agencies is of limited value in avoiding the effects of the Inland Revenue's clamp-down and is not the panacea which some commentors have suggested. However, depending on the terms of the agency contract, using agencies will continue to suit construction companies in a number of ways. It is important to weigh up the advantages and disadvantages of such schemes in each individual case.

4.4.2. Personal service companies

An individual contractor may operate through a company known as a personal service company, whereby the company will provide the services of the individual and nothing else. In operating through a limited company, subcontractors provide and are paid for work in the name of the company. Rather than drawing a salary from the personal service company, the subcontractor, as a shareholder, pays himself by way of a dividend out of the profits of the company. Dividends are not subject to NICs. There are also other tax advantages which the individual may be able to obtain from this structure.

However, merely operating through a personal service company does not necessarily ensure that a worker is a subcontractor in the Inland Revenue's eyes. The Inland Revenue will look at whether the personal service company serves any commercial purpose other than the evasion of PAYE and NICs. If the arrangements are deemed to be artificial, the Inland Revenue will collect any PAYE and NICs which have not been deducted, plus penalties and interest. The Inland Revenue may also argue that a subcontractor operating through a personal service company is merely an employee of that company and seek to recover PAYE and NICs from the company in any event. The Inland Revenue is pledged[15] to counter tax evasion in the area of personal service companies. Monies paid to a personal service company should now be treated as paid to the worker in a form that is subject to Schedule E income tax and Class 1 NICs if the worker is, in reality, an employee. Issues such as the way in which the limited company contracts, invoices, tenders, pays VAT and accepts business risks are all relevant in determining the status of the worker.[16] While the Inland Revenue's main objective in this area is the information and technology industry, the same principles may be applied by inspectors to the construction industry.

4.4.3. Partnerships

This scheme seeks to take advantage of the fact that the partners in a partnership are not employees but are self-employed. Therefore, if there is a true partnership, the partners only pay Class 2 and maybe Class 4 NICs and no PAYE. For example, a bricklaying gang, consisting of a ganger and three bricklayers, could set themselves up as a partnership. Each of the gang members would be a partner in the partnership with their relative importance in the partnership reflected by their respective share of the profits of the partnership.

However, in considering the scheme, account must again be taken of the risk that the Inland Revenue may claim that the scheme was set up for the sole purpose of evading PAYE and NICs. As with personal service companies, the Inland Revenue's announcement IR35 will have a similar effect on partnerships where the partnership will be responsible for accounting for Schedule E tax and Class 1 NICs if the partners are deemed, in reality, to be employees. Furthermore, to operate a partnership properly involves a number of complex legal and tax considerations. The workers who are to establish the partnership would need sufficient business acumen to deal with these issues. They should draft a proper partnership deed; profits will have to be shared in accordance with the terms of the deed. The partners will not only share the profits between themselves, they will also be personally liable without limit if any liabilities or debts are incurred by the partnership which cannot be met from the assets of the partnership. This is unlike a limited liability company structure whose liability is limited to the value of its share capital. A large degree of mutual trust will be required for the partnership to operate properly. All these complexities suggest that a partnership may not be appropriate in many cases; these issues may outweigh the merits of seeking to circumvent the impact of the clamp-down.

None of the schemes mentioned above can be used as a fail-safe way to avoid the impact of the clamp-down. While operating through different vehicles in different circumstances can be appropriate, the Inland Revenue will increasingly seek to look behind the schemes to expose the reality of the situation.

4.5. The Construction Industry Scheme

Not only has the industry had to deal with the clamp-down but, with effect from 1 August 1999,[17] a new scheme for taxing the industry was put in place, the Construction Industry Scheme (CIS).[18] Issues such as the classification of workers' status (as discussed above) are central to the operation of the CIS.

The CIS was introduced because the Inland Revenue was of the view that, despite the clamp-down, there was still a substantial underpayment of tax within the industry. A number of individual contractors were not properly accounting for tax due to the relative ease in obtaining 714 certificates and SC60 tax vouchers. The CIS introduced more stringent conditions before a worker in the industry is entitled to be paid without deduction of tax. This allows the Inland Revenue to collect more tax at source with the worker having to claw back any overpayment at the end of the tax year. The scheme applies to businesses in the construction industry who deal with 'Contractors' and 'Subcontractors' (as defined). 'Contractors' for the purposes of the CIS do not merely include construction companies and building firms but also government departments and local authorities. Private households and businesses which spend less than £1 million a year on construction work are not 'Contractors' and are outside the scope of the scheme. 'Subcontractors' are those businesses that carry out construction work for contractors.

In essence, for a subcontractor to be entitled to receive his payment without deduction of tax he must still obtain a tax certificate (as he did under the old 714 Scheme) but now he has to satisfy more onerous conditions in order to obtain his certificate and to receive his payment gross. A former 714 certificate holder will apply for a tax certificate, either a CIS5 or CIS6. Old 714I and 714P certificates are equivalent to a CIS6 certificate for subcontractors under the new scheme, while a 714C certificate under the old scheme is equivalent to a CIS5 certificate for companies under the new scheme. To successfully obtain a tax certificate (either a CIS5 or a CIS6)[19] not only must a worker show that he is a self-employed subcontractor[20] but also he must pass all of the following three tests

- business
- compliance
- turnover.

The main difference between qualification for a 714 certificate as compared with a CIS6 or CIS5 certificate is the turnover test requirement. If a contractor fails to get a tax certificate, he will obtain a registration card (CIS4). The significant effect of this is that even though the worker may be a subcontractor he will have income tax deducted at source through PAYE.[21]

4.5.1. Business test

A subcontractor must be able to show that his business: -

- carries out construction work in the UK or provides labour for such work
- operates through a bank account
- runs with proper records
- runs from proper premises with proper stock, equipment and other facilities.

Whether a business operates from proper premises with proper stock depends on the nature and scope of the subcontractor's work and the Inland Revenue state that they will take this into account when considering this part of the test.

4.5.2. Compliance test

Here, the subcontractor must show that, for three years ending with the date on which the application is made, he had done the following

- completed all tax returns sent to the subcontractor
- supplied any information which the tax office has requested

- paid all tax due from the subcontractor's business
- paid all the subcontractor's NICs
- paid any PAYE tax and NICs due from the subcontractor as an employer
- paid any deductions due from the subcontractor as a contractor in the construction industry.

Under the CIS the subcontractor must be able to show the Inland Revenue that he has done this all of the time and it will not be enough for the subcontractor to merely bring his affairs up to date.

4.5.3. Turnover test

Broadly, under the new CIS provisions, a company, firm or individual trader who applies for a tax certificate (CIS5/CIS6) must meet certain criteria for a continuous period of three years within the four years immediately prior to the application.

(a) A partnership or company must be able to demonstrate an annual turnover within the scheme of £30 000 (net of the cost of materials) multiplied by the number of partners/directors — the standard test; or

(b) An individual trader must be able to demonstrate an annual turnover within the scheme of £30 000 (net of the cost of materials) the standard test; or

(c) A partnership or company must be able to demonstrate an annual income of at least £200 000 (net of the cost of materials) — the alternative test. For this test, the total construction income may be included.

Contractors can make use of the 'averaging rule' and the 'six-month test' to limit the onerous nature of the turnover test.

In both the standard and alternative tests, the averaging rule means that a subcontractor will meet the test if his average annual net turnover across the three consecutive years in the four years leading up to the application is

- at least 90% of the threshold for the three years
- for two of the three years, the threshold was met.

Therefore, a sole trader will pass the turnover test if for three consecutive years his turnover was £30 000, £30 000 and £21 000. The total for the three years is £81 000 which is 90% of £90 000. To meet the alternative test, a partnership or company, regardless of the number of partners or 'Relevant Persons',[22] would have to show a net turnover from construction work of at least £200 000 in two of the three years, and at least £140 000 in the other year, to give an average of £180 000 over the three years.

The Inland Revenue has recognised that new businesses will not be able to meet any of the three year tests. The 'six-month test' means that a subcontractor will be able to obtain a certificate if he can show that his business has a net turnover from construction work of at least 70% of the annual £30 000 threshold (i.e. £21 000) in a period of no more than six consecutive income tax months in the 12 months up to the date of the application (the tax month runs from the 6th of one month to the 5th of the next).

For a two-man partnership, the partnership would have to show a turnover of at least £42 000 in the same period. However, the Inland Revenue has made it clear that until a tax certificate is issued, the new business will have to use a registration card and receive payments after deduction. This will obviously affect the cashflow of the new business.

Partnerships and companies may be able to enjoy the extra statutory concession in connection with applications which use the standard test up to 31 July 2001 to allow them to use the number of partners or Relevant Persons respectively in the business in the last six months of the three-year test period. This will assist companies and partnerships who have suffered a reduction in the number of persons involved in the business.

Where a subcontractor obtains a certificate by passing any of the three-year tests, the certificate will normally be valid for three years. If the certificate is obtained by passing the six-month test, it will be valid for one year only.

Table 4 summarises information about the turnover tests.

4.5.4. Issues in relation to the CIS

Increase in administration costs for CIS6 holders
Under the CIS, an employer may only pay a subcontractor without
deduction if the employer is satisfied that the subcontractor's tax
certificate is valid. This requirement can cause a CIS6 holder
problems in that the CIS6 certificate must carry a photograph of
the company director on its face. In order to satisfy the employer
that his CIS6 is valid and to receive payment, the director himself
must present his card with his photograph on it to the employer in
person. This may mean that directors of subcontractors holding
CIS6 certificates will be required to attend a number of sites around
the country to receive payment from employers. The answer is to
try to obtain a CIS5 certificate (the equivalent of the old 714C)
which is issued to the company or partnership as a whole and not to
any one individual. As such the holder of a CIS5 does not have to
attend site to receive payment. Unfortunately, the conditions for
getting a CIS5 certificate are stricter than for a CIS6, making it
more difficult to obtain a CIS5 certificate than it was to obtain a
714C under the 714 Scheme. CIS5s will only be issued to and
renewed to the following categories

- public companies listed on the Stock Exchange or 50%+
  subsidiaries of such companies
- companies with an annual turnover of at least £3 000 000;[23] or
- companies that can show that operating with the normal
  company certificate CIS6 (the old 714P) would cause
  substantial difficulties. Applicants in this category have to
  show a business case setting out the need for a CIS5. A
  subcontractor would have to show either
    - an administrative need in that either it generated a high
      volume of vouchers or a lot of time was spent travelling
      specifically to present a CIS6 certificate. By 'high volume
      of vouchers' the Inland Revenue would expect something

Table 4. Turnover tests

Test	Individual traders	Partnerships	Companies
Standard test: Average annual net turnover for 3 consecutive years within the four years to the date of application is at least 90% of the thresholds for those three years; and, for two years, annual net turnover was over annual threshold.	£30000 per year (i.e. at least £27000 per year over three years, and two years over £30000)	£30000 times the number of partners (i.e. at least £27000 per partner per year over three years and two years over £30000)	£30000 times number of 'Relevant Persons' (i.e. at least £27000 per year per relevant person over three years and two years over £30000)
Six Month test: Net turnover of at least 70% of the threshold for six consecutive months in the 12 months prior to the application.	£30000 per annum for six months (i.e. at least £21000 per annum for six months)	£30000 times number of partners (i.e. at least £21000 per partner per annum for six months)	£30000 times number of 'Relevant Persons' (i.e. at least £21000 per annum per relevant person for six months)
Alternative test: Average annual net turnover for three consecutive years within the four years to the date of application is at least 90% of the thresholds for those three years; and, for two years, annual net turnover was over the annual threshold.	N/A	£200000 per year (i.e. at least £180000 per annum over three years, with two years over £200000)	£200000 per year (i.e. at least £180000 per annum over three years, with two years over £200000.)

in the order of 300 vouchers per year. By 'a lot of time travelling' the Inland Revenue would need to see that at least 200 hours over the last three years or 100 hours in any one year were spent travelling solely to present a CIS6 certificate. Specific details as to the travel times, the addresses of the paying offices and the directors involved would be required to accompany the application; or

o a commercial need in that the subcontractor's trade is largely based on work for contractors who give work only to CIS5 holders.

A significant number of contracting companies will not qualify to obtain a CIS5 which will add a significant administrative burden to some contracting companies.

Increase in the amount of paperwork for CIS6 holders
Up until 6 May 2000, CIS6 holders had to complete a voucher CIS24 to be able to receive payment gross. The CIS24 showed details of the payment made. The voucher, which has three parts, was then sent to the contractor who completed further information on it before returning the subcontractor's copy to the subcontractor. Following changes announced in the Budget on 21 March 2000, this process was streamlined, having been recognised as inefficient. From 6 May 2000 a subcontractor is no longer required to send its CIS24 voucher to the contractor to merely have it returned. The subcontractor is simply required to remove their copy of the voucher and retain it for their records. The remaining two parts are then sent to the contractor as before.

Loss of interest/cashflow problems
For those subcontractors who do not qualify for a CIS5 or CIS6, and operate under a CIS4 registration card, lower rate income tax will be deducted at source even if they can show that they are self-employed subcontractors. It will be for the subcontractor then to recoup any overpayment of tax at the end of the financial year and to bear the cashflow detriment.

Increase in bogus self-employed workers

The subcontractors are not expected to produce evidence that they have been paying taxes correctly but will only have to provide a National Insurance number to obtain a CIS4. However, those without a National Insurance number will be given a CIS4 card valid for three months. This has raised fears from some areas because of the ease with which a CIS4 can be obtained. Some unscrupulous employers may pressurise workers into bogus self-employment by obtaining a CIS4 certificate rather than put them on the books as a recognised employee.

Discrimination against small subcontractors

As a result of the increase in an employer's administrative responsibilities in engaging a subcontractor who holds a CIS4 certificate, it is feared that some employers will only contract out work to those with CIS6 and CIS5 certificates. To pay a subcontractor holding a CIS4 certificate an employer not only must pay and work out the tax but is also required to complete and send in the requisite voucher, record the subcontractor's National Insurance number, provide proof of payment and give details of the work done. Small subcontractors fear that the administration involved in taxing subcontractors at source may create too much of a burden for employers.

Conflict between statutory and contractual obligations

Under the legislation, an employer can be liable to a fine of up to £3000 and loss of its own tax certificate if it improperly pays a subcontractor without a valid certificate or card.[24] However, employers are likely to be contractually bound to pay subcontractors who have undertaken work for them. As such, there is a conflict between an employer's duty to pay under the contract and to withhold payment under the legislation. To avoid such difficulties, it is advisable to ensure that within an employer's contract with a subcontractor, provision is made expressly to allow the employer to delay payment to a subcontractor in the event that the subcontractor does not satisfy the employer as to the validity of its CIS card or certificate. It is also advisable to include within the drafting an obligation on the subcontractor not only to obtain the requisite card or certificate but also to keep the employer informed as to any changes or expiry of any certificate or card after the employer's initial inspection.

Tardiness of the Inland Revenue

Many employers and subcontractors have complained that the Inland Revenue have been slow in turning round applications for registration cards and tax certificates. The Inland Revenue advised[25] that applicants should allow at least one month for tax offices to process applications. A warning was given that in complex cases (i.e. partnership or company applications where the partners' or directors' affairs have to be reviewed, joint applications or cases where the facts are difficult to establish) examination may take much longer. The combination of the rush of late applications faced by the Inland Revenue in the lead up to August 1999, and the apparent administrative delays in turning round applications, had a significant bearing on the Inland Revenue's decision to delay the full implementation of the CIS until November 1999.

See figs 3, 4 and 5 for reproductions of the CIS4(P) registration card, the CIS5 and CIS6 certificates and the associated tax vouchers and annual return forms.

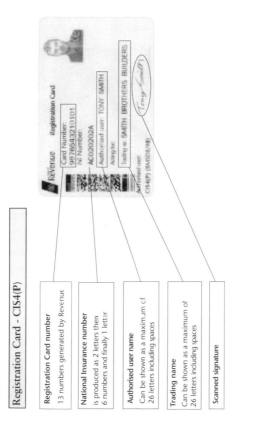

Fig. 3. CIS4 Construction Tax Certificate

79

Tax Payment Voucher - CIS25

CIS25(I) is for Impact printers,
CIS25(M) for manual completion and
CIS25(E) for EDI users

If you are using a computer and Impact printer to complete your vouchers you must start the series of
characters in the first box on each line.

You can ignore the individual boxes as in the example, although you should not use more characters than the
number of boxes on each line. The individual boxes are required for hand written vouchers. In the 'Amount
deducted' box begin the pence after the shaded box as in the example

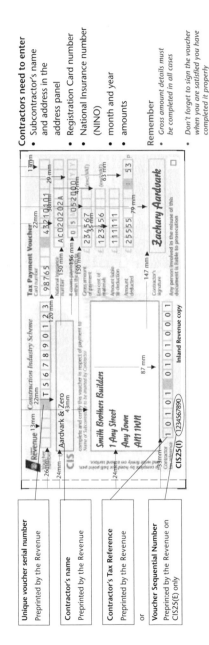

Contractors need to enter

- Subcontractor's name
  and address in the
  address panel

- Registration Card number

- National Insurance number
  (NINO)

- month and year

- amounts

Remember

- *Gross amount details must
  be completed in all cases*

- *Don't forget to sign the voucher
  when you are satisfied you have
  completed it properly*

Unique voucher serial number

Preprinted by the Revenue

Contractor's name

Preprinted by the Revenue

Contractor's Tax Reference

Preprinted by the Revenue

or

Voucher Sequential Number

Preprinted by the Revenue on
CIS25(E) only

Fig. 3. Continued. CIS25 Tax Payment Voucher

80

End of Year Return - CIS36(Transition)

Continuation Sheet completion from 1 August 1999

List all the Subcontractors holding CIS4s on one set of CIS4s on one set of CIS36(Transition) continuation sheets as shown below

Complete Part B (this side) for the period from 1 August 1999 to 5 April 2000
Complete Part A (overleaf) for the period from 6 April 1999 to 31 July 1999

Contractor's Annual Return
Continuation Sheet (Part B)

If you need more continuation sheets for Part B you should photocopy this side before you start it (or contact the Orderline on 0845 3000 551 for more forms)

If you have received approval to file vouchers electronically you must complete Part A but the Continuations Sheet for Part B for the period 1 August 1999 to 5 April 2000 should be sent by EDI.

Part B — *List of Subcontractors for period 1 August 1999 to 5 April 2000*

Column 1 Subcontractor's name	Column 2 Card or Certificate Number	Column 3 Complete in all cases	Column 4 Complete for Registration Card holders only.	Column 5 Complete for Registration Card holders only.
Enter the name of every subcontractor to whom you made payments during the tax year. Use a separate sheet for • Companies holding CIS5s • Subcontractors holding CIS6s • Subcontractors holding Registration Cards CIS4s	Enter the card number or certificate number (shown at the top of the latest CIS4, CIS5 or CIS6) produced by the subcontractor. Do not enter the National Insurance number	Enter total payments made in full without deduction of tax. Do not include VAT Do not include pence	Enter the total amount, if any, which you are satisfied represents the cost of materials used by the subcontractor under the contract.	Enter the amount deducted on the copy CIS25 Tax Payment Voucher.
		£	£	£
Smith Brothers Builders	9 8 7 6 5 4 3 2 1 0 1 0 1	234567	123456	2555553
Masons Construction	3 2 1 4 5 6 1 5 2 0 1 0 1	2295	956	30797
William Branston	5 4 3 2 1 0 9 8 7 6 1 0 1	9854	0	226442
Carry forward to Part B of CIS36(Transition) ►		246716	124412	28127 92

CIS36 Transition(CS) Part B (BMCS36(A)/99)

Contractors need to:

- **Column 1**
  tick the box for subcontractors with CIS4s and list their names
- **Column 2**
  show the Registration Card number
- **Column 3**
  show payments, in pounds only, before deduction of tax
- **Column 4**
  show the cost of materials for this contract only
- **Column 5**
  show the amount deducted and remember to include the pence

then

- total each column
- transfer details to Part B of the return CIS36(Transition)

These documents are representational as at the time of going to print, and may be subject to change

CIS62(A) (BMSD6/99)

Fig. 3. Continued.   CIS36 End of Year Return

81

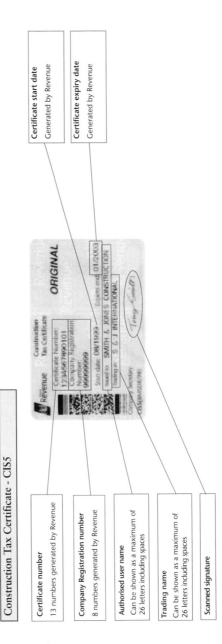

Fig. 4. CIS5 Subcontractors Tax Certificate

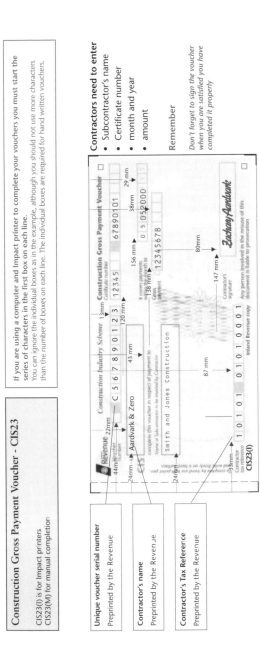

Construction Gross Payment Voucher - CIS23

CIS23(I) is for Impact printers
CIS23(M) for manual completion

If you are using a computer and Impact printer to complete your vouchers you must start the series of characters in the first box on each line.

You can ignore the individual boxes as in the example, although you should not use more characters than the number of boxes on each line. The individual boxes are required for hand written vouchers.

Contractors need to enter
- Subcontractor's name
- Certificate number
- month and year
- amount

Remember

Don't forget to sign the voucher when you are satisfied you have completed it properly

Unique voucher serial number
Preprinted by the Revenue

Contractor's name
Preprinted by the Revenue

Contractor's Tax Reference
Preprinted by the Revenue

Fig. 4. Continued. CIS23 Gross Payment Voucher

83

End of Year Return - CIS36(Transition)

Continuation Sheet completion from 1 August 1999

List all the Subcontractors holding CIS5s on one set of CIS36(Transition) continuation sheets as shown below

Complete Part B (*this side*) for the period from 1 August 1999 to 5 April 2000
Complete Part A (*overleaf*) for the period from 6 April 1999 to 31 July 1999

Contractor's Annual Return
Continuation Sheet (Part B)

If you need continuation sheets for Part B you should photocopy this side before you start it or contact the Orderline on 0845 3000 551 for more forms)

If you have received approval to file the vouchers electronically you may must complete 'Part A but the Continuation Sheet for Part B for the period 1 August 1999 to 5 April 2000 should be sent by EDI.

Part B — Total Subcontractors for period 1 August 1999 to 5 April 2000

Column 1 Subcontractor's name	Column 2 Card or Certificate Number	Column 3 Complete in all cases	Column 4 Complete in all cases	Column 5 Complete for Registration Card holders only
Enter the name of every subcontractor to whom you made payments during the tax year. Use a separate sheet for • Companies holding CIS5s • Subcontractors holding CIS6s • Subcontractors holding Registration Cards CIS4	Enter the card and number or certificate number (shown at the top of the latest CIS4, CIS5 or CIS6) produced by the subcontractor. Do not enter the National Insurance number	Enter total payments made in full without deduction of tax. Do not include VAT Do not include pence	Enter the total amount, if any, which you are satisfied represents the cost of materials used by the subcontractor under the contract. £	Enter the total amount deducted on the copy CIS25 Tax Payment Voucher. £
(tick only one box)		£	£	£
Smith & Jones Construction	1 2 3 4 5 6 7 8 9 0 1 0 1	1 2 3 4 5 6 7 8		
Johnson & Co	3 1 1 4 6 6 1 5 2 0 1 0 1	2 3 9 5		
Fred Mason Builders	5 4 3 2 1 0 9 8 7 6 1 0 1	9 6 6		

Carry forward to **Part B** of CIS36(Transition) ►   1 2 3 4 9 0 3 9

CIS36(Transition)(CS) Part B (BMX09/6/99)

Contractors need to:

- **Column 1**
  tick the box for subcontractors with CIS5s and list their names
- **Column 2**
  show the Certificate number
- **Column 3**
  show payments in pounds only
- **Column 4**
  should be left blank
- **Column 5**
  should be left blank

then

- total column 3
- transfer details to Part B, of the return CIS36(Transition)

Fig. 4. Continued. CIS36 End of Year Return

Certificate start date
Generated by Revenue

Certificate expiry date
Generated by Revenue

Acting for name
Can be shown as a maximum of 26 letters including spaces

Subcontractors Tax Certificate - CIS6

Certificate number
13 numbers generated by Revenue
(Make a record of this number for
End of Year Return completion)

National Insurance number
Produced as 2 letters then
6 numbers and finally 1 letter

Authorised user name
Can be shown as a maximum of
26 letters including spaces

Trading name
Can be shown as a maximum of
26 letters including spaces

Scanned signature

Fig. 5. CIS6 Registration Card

Subcontractors Gross Payment Voucher - CIS24

CIS24 is for manual completion only

Unique voucher serial number
Preprinted by the Revenue

Subcontractor's name
Preprinted by the Revenue

Reference number (1st ten digits of Certificate number)
Preprinted by the Revenue

National Insurance number
Preprinted by the Revenue

Subcontractors need to enter
- Contractor's name
- month and year
- gross amount

Don't forget to sign the voucher when you are satisfied you have completed it properly

Contractors need to enter
- their 10 character tax reference together with their Scheme Identification number *(this is a 3 digit number such as '001')*

Fig. 5. Continued. CIS24 Gross Payment Voucher

86

End of Year Return - CIS36(Transition)

Continuation Sheet completion from 1 August 1999

List all the Subcontractors holding CIS6s on one set of CIS36(Transition) continuation sheets as shown below

Note:
Total all payments made to a company or partnership and enter the highest Certificate number recorded for that company or partnership (see the entry for Certificate number above).

Example
There are 5 partners at Joe Jones & Sons. The highest certificate number recorded was 3114661520105. This number is then entered in column 2. You do not need to include 3114661520101 to 3114661520104

Contractor's Annual Return
Continuation Sheet (Part B)

Complete Part B, this side, for the period from 6 April 1999 to 5 April 2000

Complete Part A (overleaf) for the period from 6 April 1999 to 31 July 1999

If you need more continuation sheets for Part B you should photocopy this side before you start it (or contact the Orderline on 0845 3000 551 for more forms)

If you have received approval to file vouchers electronically you must complete Part A but the Continuation Sheet for Part B for the period 1 August 1999 to 5 April 2000 should be sent by EDI.

Column 1	Column 2	Column 3	Column 4	Column 5
Subcontractor's name	Card or Certificate Number	Complete in all cases	Complete for Registration Card holders only.	
Enter the name of every subcontractor to whom you made payments during the tax year. Use a separate sheet for: • Companies holding CIS6s • Subcontractors holding CIS6s • Subcontractors holding Registration Card CIS4s	Enter the card number or certificate number (shown at the top of the latest CIS4, CIS5 or CIS6) produced by the subcontractor Do not enter the National Insurance number	Enter total payments made in full without deduction of tax. Do not include VAT Do not include pence	Enter the total amount, if any, which you are satisfied represents the cost of materials used by the subcontractor under the contract.	Enter the total amount deducted on the copy CIS25 Tax Payment Voucher.
		£	£	£
Smith & Jones Construction	5 4 3 2 1 0 9 8 7 6 1 0 1	1 2 3 4 5 6		
Joe Jones & Sons	3 1 1 4 6 6 1 5 2 0 1 0 5	9 5		
Bill Brown Builder	1 2 3 4 5 6 7 8 9 0 1 0 3	9 5 6		

CIS36(Transition)(CS) Part B (BMT/07/HLM)   Carry forward to **Part B** of CIS36(Transition) ►   1 2 4 5 0 7

Contractors need to:

• **Column 1**
tick the box for subcontractors with CIS6s and list their names

• **Column 2**
show the Certificate number

• **Column 3**
show payments in pounds only

• **Column 4**
should be left blank

• **Column 5**
should be left blank

then

• total column 3

• transfer details to Part B, of the return CIS36(Transition)

Fig. 5. Continued.   CIS36 End of Year Return

87

NOTES

1. see the discussion in Chapter 1
2. subject always to the Inland Revenue's right to collect income tax at source under the CIS
3. later put back to 6 April 1997
4. 6 April 1997
5. see Chapter 2
6. most notably IR148, IR56 and CA69
7. 6 April 1997
8. most notably IR56, IR148 and CA69
9. see Chapter 2
10. see *Carmichael* v. *National Power plc* and *Express and Echo* v. *Tanton*
11. as confirmed in cases such as *Furniss (HMIT)* v. *Dawson, WT Ramsey Ltd* v. *Inland Revenue Commissioners* and *Craven (HMIT)* v. *White*
12. effective from 6 April 1998
13. as a result of the Inland Revenue's interpretation of section 560 of the ICTA 1998
14. see *Costain Building & Engineering Ltd* v. *Smith*
15. see leaflet IR35
16. see the Inland Revenue February 2000 Tax Bulletin guidance notes: *Provision of Personal Services through Intermediaries*
17. although the Inland Revenue extended the enforced application of the CIS by allowing certain transitional arrangements to 5 November 1999
18. The new legislation is set out in sections 559–567 of the Income and Corporation Taxes Act 1998 (ICTA) and the Income Tax (Sub-contractors in the Construction Industry) (Amendment) Regulations 1998 No. 2622.
19. see remainder of section for a discussion of the merits of a CIS5 as compared with a CIS6
20. see Chapter 2
21. As from 6 April 2000, the deduction rate was reduced from 23% to 18% (Government Press Release dated 25 February 2000)
22. 'Relevant Persons' means directors and, if the company is close (that is, broadly, controlled by five or fewer people), shareholders.
23. As from 21 March 2000, following the announcement in the Budget. This figure was reduced from £5 000 000 in recognition of the difficulties some contracting businesses faced in meeting the business case.
24. see Sections 566(2A) and (2B) of ICTA
25. leaflet IR40(CIS)

5

Working time

When faced with a tight deadline on a construction project, increasing the number of man-hours which are deployed on the project can be an effective way of accelerating progress. However, employers face a number of legal constraints which limit the extent to which the workforce can be required to increase their working hours, namely

- health and safety legislation on working time
- contractual and regulatory holiday entitlement
- paternity and maternity rights
- time off whilst sick
- time off for family emergencies
- time off for certain extra curricular activities which have been considered to be for the greater good.

All of the above give workers in the industry the right to take time off work in certain circumstances, be it paid or unpaid. What is common to all workers of whatever status is that an employer must look beyond the worker's contractual rights and in addition consider the worker's statutory rights in order to see the full picture of the worker's entitlement to time off work. This chapter concentrates on one aspect of these rights which gives rise to particular issues in the industry, namely the regulation of working time.

As discussed in Chapter 1, an employer is obliged to include a statement regarding an employee's hours of work and holiday entitlement in the employee's written statement of particulars. The collective agreements discussed in Chapter 3 set out the hours of work, minimum rest breaks and contractual holiday to which workers covered by those agreements are entitled. While the relevant working rule agreements make use of the various derogations provided for in the Working Time Regulations 1998 (the Regulations),[1] the Regulations are nevertheless the source of a large proportion of the statutory rights which apply in addition to a worker's contractual entitlements.

5.1. Working Time Regulations 1998

The Regulations came into force on 1 October 1998 and have caused significant problems in the industry. They were introduced by reason of the requirement to introduce into English law the provisions of two European Union directives,[2] both of which derive from European Union health and safety policy. As such, the Regulations must be interpreted purposively by courts and tribunals, to give effect to the health and safety objectives which underlie the directives.

The Regulations introduced new entitlements for 'workers' to

- a maximum 48-hour working week
- minimum rest breaks
- paid annual leave
- special entitlements for night workers (including an entitlement to a health assessment and the transfer to day work in certain circumstances).

5.1.1. Scope of protection

The Regulations apply to workers rather than just to employees. Regulation 2(1) states that a 'worker' is:

> somebody employed under a contract of employment or any other contract whereby the individual undertakes to do or perform personally any work or services for another party to the contract whose status is not by virtue of the contract that of client or customer of any profession or business undertaking carried on by the individual.

When applied in the construction industry, the status of so-called independent contractors is once again called into question. The DTI Guidance which accompanies the Regulations and the amended Guidance published on 31 March 2000 states that the term 'worker' will cover those individuals employed under a contract of employment as well as other individuals to whom an employer has a duty to provide work, who controls when and how it is done, supplies tools and other equipment and pays tax and NICs. No guidance is given as to what is meant by 'performing personally any work'. The guidance states that a worker will include agency workers and freelance workers but will not extend to self-employed people who are genuinely pursuing a business activity on their own account.

The decision of the Ashford Employment Tribunal in *Willoughby v. County Home Care Ltd* examined the definition of 'worker' in the case of a healthcare worker. Under her contract she was not entitled to sick or holiday pay; she could not be disciplined under a disciplinary procedure; she was not obliged to accept work, neither did she have an entitlement to be provided with work. The Tribunal found that, notwithstanding these factors which led to the conclusion that the worker was not an employee, she was, nevertheless, a 'worker' for the purposes of the Regulations. The Tribunal held that the care worker was not an employee due to the lack of mutuality of obligation in respect of offering and accepting work. However, as the care worker had agreed to do the work personally and there was no right to delegate the work to a third party, she fell within the definition of a 'worker' under Regulation

2(1). The extent to which a similar conclusion would be reached in respect of any given worker in the construction industry will depend upon the nature of the worker's engagement.

This raises the question of how an employer who hires an independent contractor can ensure that the independent contractor does not have 'worker' status under the Regulations. The answer may be for the employer to specify in the contract that the independent contractor is not required to work or to provide services personally. In such circumstances employers would be well advised to insert an express provision to that effect into their contracts, provided that such a provision would be consistent with the work which the independent contractor has been hired to do. This strategy appears to have been partially endorsed by the Court of Appeal in the case of *Express & Echo Publications Ltd* v. *Tanton*, a case concerning the definition of an employee. Despite the trend of previous decisions[3] which called for an analysis of what happens in practice rather than a reliance on the contract terms and the labels given by the parties, the Court of Appeal in *Express & Echo* held that if the contract contains a term that is incompatible with the relationship of employer and employee, the individual cannot be considered an employee. While this case concerned the definition of an 'employee' as opposed to a 'worker', it provides a useful analysis of the importance of contract terms in defining the relationship. It lends support to the suggestion that a provision whereby the independent contractor does not have to perform the services personally will ensure that he does not acquire the status of 'worker' for the purposes of Regulations. Having said that, the courts and tribunals are bound to look to the purpose of the Regulations when deciding such questions. When there is any element artificially attempting to place a given person into a given category, such manoeuvring must be treated with circumspection.

5.1.2. The Maximum '48-hour week'

Regulation 4(1) provides that a worker's average working week shall not exceed 48 hours. The High Court held in *Barber & Others*

v. *RJB Mining (UK) Ltd* that the right in Regulation 4(1) not to have to work in excess of a maximum of 48 hours on average in any week is a free standing legal right, enforceable as an obligation of the employer under the worker's contract of employment or contract for services. As such, when several miners were instructed to work more than the maximum, the High Court issued a declaration that the miners were entitled to refuse to continue working in excess of the limit.

The average number of weekly working hours is calculated over a 17-week reference period and includes mandatory overtime hours (that is, overtime which a worker is contractually obliged to undertake). In some construction companies, this can include half days on Saturdays. If a worker has fixed hours of work (i.e. 9.30 am to 5.00 pm) voluntary overtime is not included in calculating the number of weekly working hours where the employer has not required the worker to perform the work.[4] The Regulations permit the reference period to be extended to up to 52 weeks where there are objective technical reasons, or reasons concerning the organisation of work, which justify the extension and where there is an agreement between workers and their employers to that effect. As discussed in Chapter 3, the NAECI, the JIB Agreement and the HVAC Agreement have all provided for the extension of the reference period to 52 weeks for workers engaged under the terms of those collective agreements.

Traditionally, the construction industry works longer hours in the summer than during the winter. Therefore it is conceivable that during a 17-week reference period falling within the summer, many workers would fall foul of the 48-hour rule whilst during a similar period in the winter their hours would fall within the 48-hour limit. Adopting a 52-week reference period would permit the excess and the shortfall to cancel one another out when calculating the average weekly hours over the longer reference period.

Many employers within the industry appear to be taking advantage of another way around the maximum working week, namely the derogation provided for in the Regulations which allows individual workers to opt out of the 48-hour limit. A worker may opt out of the maximum by signing a written agreement to that effect. Such an agreement (such as that shown in Fig. 6) may be terminated by the worker on not less than three months notice. Workers cannot be forced to opt out in this way but for so long as workers continue to be paid hourly rates it is likely that many workers will be prepared to opt out to maximise their earnings. This derogation will not apply after 2003.

The original drafting of the Regulations[5] obliged employers, *inter alia*, to keep records of the working time of those who had opted-out for two years. However, the Working Time Regulations 1999 have removed this requirement. Nevertheless, employers are obliged to keep for at least two years records of working time of all of those who had not opted out.[6]

Following the amendment to Regulation 20,[7] employers need only concern themselves with recording their workers' pre-determined hours of work (if the hours are fixed by, for example, a provision in their contract) and those additional hours which the workers are *required* to perform by the employer. In such circumstances, employers need not keep records of workers' voluntary overtime. Despite this relaxation of the employer's duties, employers remain obliged[8] to take all reasonable steps in keeping with the need to protect the health and safety of workers to ensure that the 48-hour maximum limit is complied with.

5.2. HOLIDAY PAY, HOLIDAY ENTITLEMENT AND TIME OFF WORK

There are two aspects to holiday entitlements — the right to time off and the right to be paid during such time off notwithstanding that no work is undertaken. Historically, such rights are a matter of contract, to be agreed between the employer and the worker. Under the industry's various working rule agreements workers are entitled to between 21 and 25 days holiday per year in addition to public holidays (21 in the CIJC Agreement and 25 in the NAECI). Traditionally, the industry has required part of this holiday

THIS AGREEMENT is made the [   ] day of [   ] 200[ ]

BETWEEN

1.   [   ] ("the Company") whose registered office is situated at

      [   ].

2.   A N OTHER of [   ]

NOW IT IS HEREBY AGREED

1.   You hereby acknowledge that the Working Time Regulations 1998 (the
      "Regulations") provide that a worker's working time, including overtime, shall
      not exceed an average of 48 hours for each seven day period. Nevertheless,
      pursuant to the provisions of the Regulations, you hereby agree that such limit
      shall not apply in your case.

2.   Clause 1 of this Agreement shall remain in force indefinitely unless and until
      terminated by you by giving to the Company not less than three months' prior
      notice in writing.

3.   In order to comply with the Regulations the Company is required to monitor the
      amount of time you spend working. To enable it to comply with such a
      requirement, you agree to comply with the monitoring arrangements imposed by
      the Company from time to time including, where necessary, the completion of
      such records as the Company considers necessary for this purpose.

4.   You confirm that not withstanding the termination of the agreement evidenced in
      Clause 1 of this Agreement, you will comply with the monitoring arrangements
      with which the Company has to comply in accordance with the Regulations and
      to that extent Clause 3 above shall continue in full force and effect.

Signed by...

Signed by ....

For and on behalf of the Company

....   Name

....   Position

....   Date

Fig. 6. Example of a waiver agreement

entitlement to be taken over the Christmas and Easter shut-down periods and in the summer.

However, the Regulations provide for a minimum entitlement for all workers who have been employed continuously for 13 weeks or more to four weeks paid annual leave.

5.2.1. Industry holidays and the Regulations

It has been common practice for the majority of construction companies to provide for holiday pay through various schemes such as

- the Building and Civil Engineering Holiday Scheme (now amended and called 'Template')
- JIB Annual Holiday with Pay Scheme
- WELPLAN Scheme.

in recognition of the itinerant nature of a large proportion of their workforce. Generally under the schemes an employer provides weekly 'credits' for each operative who has worked for him for a certain number of days during a given week. The value of the 'credits' includes an element for holiday pay which is calculated according to an operative's normal basic salary (excluding overtime payments and any additional commission or incentive payments which he may have received). When an operative takes a day's holiday he is paid under the schemes. The purpose of the schemes is to ensure that each employer of the worker throughout the year contributes a fair amount to the worker's holiday pay entitlement. While the schemes often provide other benefits (such as Death and Accident Benefits and a range of pensions for workers) they merely provide for the payment of a cash sum and do not provide a right to take paid holiday. Therefore, the amount of paid holiday workers were able to take depended entirely on their employers; the workers had no legal entitlement to demand a holiday unless such a right was contained within their contract.

Furthermore, the value of holiday credits that were paid under some of the schemes was less than the value of a 'week's pay' that employers are obliged to pay under the Regulations. Hence, participating employers would not be meeting their duties under the Regulations when they provided for holiday pay in this way. As a consequence and with effect from 1 August 1999, the Building and Civil Engineering Holiday Scheme was amended to ensure participating employees were able to comply with the Regulations.

5.2.2. Four weeks' leave

A week's leave is stated in the DTI Guidance which accompanies the Regulations to be the amount of time a worker works during a normal working week. So, for example, a worker who works five days a week is now entitled to four weeks annual leave of 20 working days. Any payment received by a worker for public holidays or other holidays to which he is entitled will count towards discharging his employer's liability under the Regulations.

5.2.3. A week's pay

The right to four weeks' paid annual holiday is limited to the right to receive a week's pay for each week of leave.[9] A week's pay is the worker's weekly contractual remuneration where the worker has a normal working week, that is to say where a worker's contract provides for particular hours of work and where the worker works those hours. Where the worker does not have a normal working week, then a week's pay will be the average weekly remuneration calculated by reference to the previous 12 weeks. The remuneration to be included in the calculation will include any salary, wages and contractual overtime payments (overtime which the worker is obliged to work), commission or bonus payments received but is unlikely to include travel allowance and subsistence payments. Once the total remuneration over the 12-week period has been calculated, the total number of hours worked over that 12-week period is ascertained. The average hourly rate can then be calculated from these two figures. A week's pay is the hourly rate multiplied by the average number of hours worked per week. The amended DTI Guidance makes it clear that pay and hours of non-compulsory overtime is excluded in the calculation.

The calculation of a week's pay is as follows

Week's pay = Average number of hours worked per week *multiplied by* hourly rate

Hourly rate = Salary *plus* bonus *plus* commission *plus* contractual overtime at higher rate (but not non-contractual overtime) received over 12 weeks

Divided by

Total number hours worked, including contractual but not non-compulsory overtime hours over 12 weeks

Prior to its revision, problems arose under the Building and Civil Engineering Benefit Schemes (the Scheme) because the method of calculation of holiday pay under the Scheme was on an entirely different basis to that prescribed in the Regulations. Whereas the Scheme used basic salary only, the Regulations take into account contractual overtime, commission and bonus payments. The disparity between the two calculation methods meant that those workers who received holiday pay under the Scheme were unlikely to receive their full entitlement to holiday pay as provided for under the Regulations. To the extent that there was any shortfall in payment under the Scheme, employers had to ensure that they topped up those payments.

5.2.4. Template scheme

On 2 August 1999, Building and Civil Engineering Holidays Scheme Management Ltd launched its holiday pay plan 'Template' which allows employers to meet their obligations under the Construction Industry Joint Council Working Rule Agreement and the Regulations. Template has heralded a move from the holiday credits system to a hybrid, which allows payments to operatives for holidays from the contributions the employer has made to

Template. However, the obligation as to the level of holiday pay each worker is entitled to is left firmly with the employer. In so far as the payments that a worker receives from Template are less than the worker's entitlement under the Regulations, the employer remains responsible to top these up.

5.2.5. Employer's notices

It remains possible under the Regulations for employers to dictate to a degree when workers must take their annual leave entitlement.[10] Clearly this will be desirable in the construction industry where there are long established and traditional shut-down periods. Furthermore, it can also be used by an employer to avoid the need to make holiday payments at an inflated rate where a worker who does not have a 'normal working week' proposes to take some holiday immediately following a 12-week period during which he has earned significant bonuses and commission payments. An employer can require his workers to take their holiday entitlement at specific times by giving them a notice specifying the days the worker is required to take. Workers must be given at least twice as many days notice as the number of days holiday. So, for example, where an employer wants a worker to take five days holiday, he must give the worker at least ten days' notice.

5.3. REST BREAKS

Construction companies are required to provide their workers with various minimum rest breaks. The Regulations provide all workers with the right to a minimum daily rest period of 11 hours in each 24-hour period, a weekly rest period of 24-hours in each 7-day period (or 48-hours over a 2-week period) and a rest period of at least 20 minutes where a worker is working for more than six hours a day.

The entitlements to daily and weekly rest periods will not apply to shift workers when they change shift and cannot take a daily rest period between the end of one shift and the start of the next. However, there is an obligation on the construction company to allow the workers to take an equivalent period of compensatory rest at an alternative time.[12] The NAECI, JIB Agreement and HVAC Agreement have all made use of the derogations contained within the Regulations[13] to exclude the regulatory rest breaks in favour of the rest breaks allowed for in each of the respective working rule agreements.

The impact of tight deadlines on construction projects may mean that it simply is not practicable to allow a particular worker to take his prescribed rest breaks. In circumstances where there is an exceptional and unforeseen surge of work the Regulations provide that rest periods can be ignored, so long as the employer provides equivalent periods of rest as soon as is reasonably practicable. Alternatively, in exceptional cases where it is not possible to do so, the employer must afford that worker 'such protection as may be appropriate to safeguard his health and safety'. The Regulations do not explain what is intended to fall within the definition of an exceptional and unforeseen surge of work, although it is submitted that as deadlines in construction projects are set in advance, there will be few circumstances when such time pressures qualify as an exceptional or unforeseen surge in work. It is likely that a heavy onus will rest with the employer to persuade a tribunal that rules laid down for the health and safety of the workers should be disapplied in a given set of circumstances.

5.4. NIGHT WORK

Where construction companies engage night workers, special provisions apply.[14] A night worker is defined as somebody who, in the normal course, works at least three hours of his daily working time during the night (a period of not less than seven hours which includes the period between midnight and 5 am). In the case of *R v. Attorney General for Northern Ireland ex parte Burns* a worker who worked at night one week in every three was held to work at night 'as a matter of course'. In the Attorney General's opinion, working at night meant no more than as a regular feature of employment. While the majority of construction workers will not be night workers, site security guards and the like may well qualify.

A night worker cannot be required to work on average more than eight hours in any 24-hour period. The reference period over which the average is taken is 17 weeks. However, where an employee's night work involves dealing with special hazards or heavy physical or mental strain he must not work more than eight hours in *any* 24-hour period.

A night worker must also have the opportunity to undergo a health assessment before he begins night work and he must also be provided with the opportunity to attend health assessments at appropriate intervals throughout the period during which he is undertaking night work.[15]

5.5. ENFORCEMENT

Rights under the Regulations can be enforced in three ways[16]

- via the Health and Safety Executive, which is the relevant enforcement agency with wide powers of investigation
- individual workers can enforce the Regulations through employment tribunals. An employment tribunal which finds such a claim to be well-founded may make a declaration to that effect and may make an award of compensation
- following the *Barber* case (Section 5.2.1.) workers may be able to bring claims for breach of contract in the High Court or in the County Court.

A worker has the right not to be subjected to any detriment and, in the case of employees (but not workers), a right not to be unfairly dismissed for seeking to exercise his rights under the Regulations. A dismissal on the grounds that an employee has

- refused to comply with a requirement of the employer imposed in contravention of the Regulations
- refused to forego a right under the Regulations
- failed to sign a workforce agreement for the purposes of the Regulations
- been a representative or a candidate for a representative of the members of the workforce in connection with a workforce agreement; or
- brought proceedings against the employer or alleged that the employer has infringed a right under Regulations.

will be automatically unfair.[17]

NOTES

1. Regulation 23
2. the Working Time Directive (Council Directive 93/104/EC) and the Young Workers' Directive (Council Directive 93/33/EC)
3. see further the analysis in Chapter 2
4. Working Time Regulations 1999
5. Regulation 5(4)
6. Regulation 9
7. as a result of the Working Time Regulations 1999
8. by the overriding duty set out at Regulation 4(2)
9. Regulations 13 to 16 and Sections 221 to 224 of the Employment Rights Act 1996
10. Regulation 15
11. Regulations 10, 11 and 12
12. Regulation 24
13. Regulation 23
14. Regulation 6
15. Regulation 7
16. Regulation 28
17. Regulation 31 which amends Section 45 of the Employment Rights Act 1996

6

Guarantee payment, minimum wage and deductions

The payment of workers within the construction industry is determined by agreement, either individually or collectively. However, regardless of what is agreed, a framework of legislation provides protection for workers.

- Section 28 of the Employment Rights Act 1996 provides that in certain circumstances employees are entitled to guarantee payments.
- The National Minimum Wage Act 1998 provides for minimum hourly rates of pay for workers.
- Section 13 of the Employment Rights Act 1996 provides that employers can only deduct monies from a worker in certain circumstances.

6.1. GUARANTEE PAYMENT

Where work is temporarily stopped or is not provided by the employer, in certain circumstances the industry's working rule agreements allow employers to temporarily lay-off employees.[1] When an employee is laid off, rather than being made redundant, he will be entitled to a minimum fall-back payment known as a guarantee payment from his employer.[2] This entitles him to a payment calculated in accordance with the statutory formula for every workless day. The calculation of the statutory guarantee payment[3] is dependent upon the hours worked by the employee and his contract. However, it is to be noted that the maximum payment for any day is £16.10.[4] Furthermore, the number of days for which he can claim this payment is limited to an overall maximum of five days in any one period of three months. The right may be lost in some circumstances. The purpose of the enactment is to compensate the employee for the loss, incurred through no fault of his own, of what he would have earned in normal circumstances. This is payable for days which they would normally be expected to work under their contracts of employment, but throughout which the employer has not provided them with work (because of, say, inclement weather or lack of materials). Some employees are excluded from this benefit such as

- *short-term employees:* i.e. employees employed under fixed term contracts of three months or less
- *casual employees:* i.e. employees employed to perform a specific task which is not expected to take longer than three months
- *employees covered by collective contracting out:* i.e. where the Secretary of State has made an order[5] to exclude employees who are covered by a collective agreement which itself gives the employees a right to guarantee pay which is no less generous than the statutory right.

Such orders have been made in relation to a number of the industry's collective agreements. In 1997 the Working Rule Agreement of the Civil Engineering and Construction Conciliation Board was ordered as an excluded collective agreement.[6] In 1996, the then Building Employers Confederation and the National Federation of Roofing Contractors entered into an agreement with UCATT, TGWU and GMB and obtained an order excluding those employees covered by the collective agreement.[7] The Electrical Contracting and Heating & Ventilating Contractors have not obtained a similar order in relation to these collective agreements and therefore only the statutory provisions apply.

6.1.1. Statutory provisions

A 'workless day' is defined as a period of 24 hours midnight to midnight where two conditions are satisfied.

(a) During those 24 hours the employee is given no work to do at all because of one of the specified reasons
(b) In normal circumstances his contract would require him to work at least part of those 24 hours.

As such, an employee cannot claim for a day when he would have been on holiday or off sick or where he has merely lost his voluntary overtime. Similarly, an employee has no right to a guarantee payment where the failure to provide work is in consequence of an industrial dispute.

An employee will lose his right to a guarantee payment on either of two grounds.

(a) If he unreasonably refuses an offer of suitable alternative employment for the day.
(b) If he does not comply with the reasonable requirements imposed by his employer with a view to ensuring that his services are available.

6.1.2. Collective agreement provisions

The Construction Industry Joint Council, the Engineering Construction Industry, the Thermal Insulation Contracting Industry and the Heating, Ventilation, Air Conditioning, Piping and Domestic Engineering Industry all provide within their collective agreements for specific rules for guarantee payment.

These are more generous than the statutory guarantee payment in that generally the minimum weekly earnings calculation of the guarantee payments are based on normal working hours (between 38 and 39 hours) and the basic rates of pay, rather than the statutory minimum amounts. The different collective agreements have particular conditions pertaining to the particular collective agreement. For instance, the Engineering Construction Industry provides that only employees who have been continuously employed for not more than four weeks shall be entitled to a guarantee payment. No such qualification period applies in the Construction Industry Joint Council Agreement. For the Heating, Ventilation, Air Conditioning, Piping and Domestic Engineering Agreement, an employee needs to be continuously employed for not less than two weeks, while the Thermal Insulation Contracting Industry requires four weeks continuity of employment. However, all agreements are limited to a week's wages.

6.2. The National Minimum Wage

With effect from the 1 April 1999, all relevant 'workers' became entitled to the National Minimum Wage (NMW).[8]

6.2.1. The rate of the National Minimum Wage

The rates are as follows

- the main single hourly rate is £3.70 (from 1 October 2000, before which it costs £3.60)
- for those workers over 18 but less than 22, the rate is £3.20 per hour
- for those workers who are 22 or over but are within the first six months of employment with a new employer and where they are on accredited training on at least 26 days in the relevant six-month period, their hourly rate is £3.20.

The genuine self-employed, under 18-year olds, genuine volunteers and apprentices between 18 and 26 years old in the first 12 months of their apprenticeships, are exempt from the NMW. While the majority of workers in the construction industry are not immediately affected by the NMW, an understanding of the legislation is nevertheless necessary as the Low Pay Commission is obliged to review the level of the NMW and there may be some workers who perhaps are paid a modest annual salary but who do such a large number of working hours that a construction company could be in breach of the NMW.

6.2.2. The Low Pay Commission

The Low Pay Commission[9] has the central role in recommending the rate for the NMW and the basis upon which the rate should be calculated. As with the Working Time Regulations 1998, the National Minimum Wage Act 1998 is applicable to all 'workers'. The definition includes any workers who undertake to do or perform personally any work or services.

6.2.3. Calculation of the hourly rate

To ascertain whether an employer has breached the National Minimum Wage Regulations, the following needs to be considered[10]

(1) The hourly rate paid to a worker in a pay reference period shall be determined by dividing the total calculated in accordance with paragraph (2) by the number of hours specified in paragraph (3).

(2) The total referred to in paragraph (1) shall be calculated by subtracting from the total of remuneration in the pay reference period determined under Regulation 30, the total of reductions determined under Regulations 31–37.

(3) The hours referred to in paragraph (1) are the total number of hours of time work, salaried hours work, output work and unmeasured work worked by the worker in the pay reference

period that have been ascertained in accordance with Regulations 20–29.

As can be seen there are four distinct types of work identified for the purpose of calculating the total number of hours, namely time work, salaried hours work, output work and unmeasured work.

Once the total number of hours in the pay reference period have been established and the amount of remuneration has been identified, an employer is able to calculate whether he has paid an amount equivalent to the NMW. In calculating the total remuneration, all monies received by an employee within the pay reference period should be counted. One exception to this is benefits in kind (other than those in relation to accommodation).

6.2.4. Duty to keep records

While the National Minimum Wage Act 1998 does not require employers to provide a NMW statement to all workers as was proposed when the legislation was being drafted, an employer has a general obligation to keep records which are 'sufficient to establish that he is remunerating the worker at a rate at least equal to the NMW'. These records must be kept for a period of at least three years. An employer in the industry should note the importance of keeping records as the onus of showing that a worker has been paid on or above the NMW is placed on the employer.[11] Additionally, workers have a right to require an employer to produce relevant records and to inspect the same.

6.2.5. Enforcement

In addition to a worker being able to bring proceedings in his own right in an employment tribunal or through the courts, 'relevant officers who are appointed to ensure compliance' can bring proceedings on the worker's behalf. Currently, it is the Inland Revenue which is empowered to enforce the NMW.

6.3. DEDUCTION FROM WAGES

Section 13 of the Employment Rights Act 1996[12] provides protection to workers from having deductions taken from their wages. An employer may not make a deduction from any wages for any worker employed by him or receive a payment from a worker unless

- it is required or authorised to be made by virtue of any statutory provision or any relevant provision of the worker's contract; or
- the worker has previously signed in writing his agreement or consent to the making of it.

Effectively, this prohibits deductions from a worker's wages (other than income tax and national insurance contributions or in compliance with a court order) unless the worker has expressly agreed in writing.

Matters are further complicated as a result of various cases that have taken a strict interpretation of the statutory exception that a deduction can be made where a worker has signified his consent in writing. Courts and tribunals have made it clear that not only must the consent be signed by the worker and be in writing but also the consent must be drafted in sufficiently precise terms so that the worker knows exactly what amounts he may be allowing his employer to deduct from his wages and how that deduction is to be made.

A construction employer should therefore bear in mind Section 13 particularly when granting workers loans or making payments for training courses conditional upon the worker either completing the course or remaining employed with that employer for a period of time. The recoupment provisions in any such written agreement should be clear and unambiguous as to when, how and why the employer can seek to deduct monies from wages.

It is not to be forgotten that Section 13 only relates to deduction from wages. Any freestanding loan agreement or other arrangement will be enforceable in the normal way by an employer as against his worker.

NOTES

1. see Working Rule 17.4 of CIJC Agreement, section 13 of NAECI, rule 5(d)(iv) of HVAC Agreement and Rule 7 of the 'Employment Practice' of the JIB Agreement
2. pursuant to Section 28 of the Employment Rights Act 1996
3. Section 30 of the Employment Rights Act 1996
4. from 1 February 2000: SI 1999/3375
5. under Section 35 of the Employment Rights Act 1996
6. SI 1987/156
7. SI 1996/2132
8. following the introduction of the National Minimum Wage Act 1998 which is supplemented by the National Minimum Wage Regulations 1999 (SI 1999/584)
9. established by Section 8 of the National Minimum Wage Act 1998
10. Regulation 14
11. Section 28 of the National Minimum Wage Act 1998
12. which consolidates the provisions of the Wages Act 1986

7

Training

7.1. INTRODUCTION

There has been much debate within the construction industry regarding the extent to which employers within the industry ought to take responsibility for training. Factors such as the economic downturn and increased levels of subcontracting have occasioned a serious decline in construction employers' involvement with apprenticeship training since the mid-1980s.

With the introduction of training incentives for employers such as industry training grants and an increase in the requirement that operatives hold recognised qualification certificates such as those issued under the Construction Skills Certification Scheme (CSCS), the importance of training is gaining prominence.

Recognised training in the construction industry is provided by three main sources, namely

(a) industry training organisations, such as the Construction Industry Training Board (CITB) and the Engineering Construction Industry Training Board (ECITB)
(b) training and enterprise councils and local enterprise companies (government funded bodies)
(c) further education colleges.

Most of the co-ordination of training is done by the industry training organisations, which either provide the training themselves or send the trainees out to training and enterprise councils, local enterprise companies or further education colleges.

This chapter concentrates on the two statutory industry training organisations, the CITB and the ECITB. It should be noted that a number of other non-statutory bodies exist, such as Engineering Services Training Trust Ltd,[1] J T Ltd[2] and the National Electrotechnical Training Organisation.

7.2. EMPLOYERS' OBLIGATIONS

There are certain sectors of the construction industry where operatives must have received some kind of recognised training or a qualification before they are allowed on site. For example, gas installers must be registered with CORGI (The Council for Registered Gas Installers). The qualifications necessary for such registrations vary according to the type of work carried out although there is a basic requirement that everyone has a health and safety certificate. Up until last year these certificates were acquired following approved courses run by bodies such as the CITB. Now they are obtained through the new nationally Accredited Certification Scheme. These certificates have to be renewed every five years.

Not all sectors of the construction industry are subject to exacting legal training requirements such as those which apply to gas installers. However, in many cases workers will be required to have attained a certain level of qualification as a result of their employer having entered into a contractual obligation to deploy skilled and qualified workers. Workers employed on sensitive sites, such as petrochemical refinery plants, are required by contract to go through certain recognised checks. An increasing number of clients (such as local authorities, British Airports Authority, and British Nuclear Fuels Ltd) are requiring workers to be on an approved industry training programme and to carry cards to verify their skills. This is particularly so in relation to health and safety training.

The CSCS was designed to meet this requirement. It allows trained workers to apply for a CSCS Link card which lasts for three years while the worker works towards a National Vocational Qualification (NVQ) or Scottish Vocational Qualification (SVQ). If the NVQ or SVQ is not obtained within the three-year period, the card will be withdrawn. A multitude of occupations are eligible for the CSCS Link card (including painting and decorating, carpentry, joinery and bricklaying).

7.3. THE ROLES OF THE CITB AND ECITB IN TRAINING

7.3.1. CITB

The CITB was established in 1964[3] in order to improve the quality of the training and the facilities available for training in the construction industry. It ensures that the quality of training is maintained at a high level by approving courses and by setting standards which must be met in order to obtain the appropriate qualifications. It also ensures that sufficient places are available on training courses to meet the industry's needs.

The CITB is involved primarily in the training of apprentices and young workers. It provides grants to employers who take on trainees and will assist young workers in securing a job.

The CITB oversees a number of training courses, the main ones being

- the New Deal
- the National Traineeship
- the Modern Apprenticeship
- the Construction Apprentice Scheme (CAS)

as well as helping to provide funding for NVQ and SVQ courses. Although the CITB does not run many of its own adult training courses, it does provide subsidies for other organisations to provide such training.

7.3.2. ECITB

The ECITB was established in July 1991[4] in recognition of the role that the engineering construction industry plays in the UK economy. The ECITB (a registered charity) provides all aspects of training for the engineering sector of the construction industry, ranging from site skills to head office and management requirements. Its aim is to maintain a well-trained workforce at all levels.

It runs two main schemes approved by the National Joint Council for the Engineering Construction Industry leading to qualification as an engineer, namely

(a) the National Skills Development Scheme which provides employees with a route to Craftsman and Advanced Craftsman grades through training, assessment and experience
(b) the National Apprenticeship Scheme for Engineering Construction for training in the trades of erector, mechanical fitter, pipe fitter, plater and welder.

The Board, which is made up of clients, employers, trade unions and education specialists, also provides general support and advice to those in the industry.

7.4. FUNDING

Both the CITB and the ECITB are entitled[5] to raise a levy from every company[6] engaged in the construction or engineering construction industry[7] in order to fund their work. Once a levy has been raised, it is recoverable as an ordinary debt owed to the CITB/ECITB, normally by means of a claim in the County Courts. Both the CITB and ECITB only provide training grants to those companies which are registered with the CITB and ECITB respectively (to assist the CITB and ECITB in their administration) and have paid their levy up to date.

7.4.1. CITB

The CITB's levy is based on the number of people working for an employer. The current rates payable by the employer are

- 0·38% of payroll in respect of employees employed under contracts of service or apprenticeship
- 2·28% of net payments to persons under labour-only agreements (self-employed workers).

The level of the CITB levy based on payroll of employees employed under contracts of service or apprenticeship is likely to rise to 0·86% by the year 2003 as part of the CITB's five-year programme of gradual change (Vision 2000).

The funding of the CITB has been hit hard by the Inland Revenue clamp-down and the move from self-employed workers to employees, as independent subcontractors pay a higher levy than companies which employ workers directly.

Employers registered with the CITB may qualify for an exemption or a reduction in the levy. The current thresholds are

- if the total paid out in wages is less than £61 000 then the employer is fully exempt
- if the total paid out in wages is less than £100 000 then the employer makes a flat rate payment of £250 to the CITB.

All employers in the industry must file a return annually with the CITB so that their levy can be calculated.

7.4.2. ECITB

The ECITB's levy is similarly based on the wages bill. The current rates are

- 1·5% of the total emoluments (i.e. payments which are

assessable to Schedule E income tax) of all site employees and total net labour-only payments for site employees, where that sum exceeds £75 000

- 0·18% of the total emoluments of all off-site employees and the total net labour-only payments for off-site employees, where that sum exceeds £100 000.[8]

Accordingly, for those employers whose on-site and off-site wages do not exceed £75 000 and £100 000 respectively, they are exempt from the levy in view of their small number of employees.[9]

Two forms are sent to the employer every April which they must complete and return to the ECITB giving details of total revenue, staffing levels and labour-only payments.

7.5. FUNDING CRITICISMS

7.5.1. CITB

The CITB's levy is particularly unpopular and is considered by many employers to be unfair. The main criticisms are that

- only those who want to promote training register with the CITB and pay the levy
- the paperwork to calculate the levy and to apply for training grants is complex and time consuming
- too much of the money going to the CITB is used up in administration rather than for actual training.

7.5.2. ECITB

The ECITB is subjected to less criticism as the levy is seen to be more fairly distributed and a greater proportion of the funds are used solely for training.

It has been suggested that the levies should be on materials so that everyone in the industry makes some contribution to raising the standards through the means of training.

7.6. IMPROVEMENTS TO THE TRAINING SYSTEM

In 1998, the CITB published, in conjunction with the Construction Confederation, a pamphlet entitled *Training—It's our responsibility*. In an attempt to gain an industry-wide commitment to craft and management training, it suggested a shift of resources from youth programmes of craft training of 16–19 year olds[10] to a 'whole industry training culture' more applicable to employees of all ages across the industry. It listed five strategic issues

(a) Gaining employers' commitment to a whole industry training culture.
(b) The provision of an adequately funded and understandable system for construction training providing clear routes for career progression.
(c) Increasing the perception of all parties to the value of a competent workforce.
(d) Improving the image of the industry with the aim of achieving better quality recruits at all levels.
(e) The achievement of policy coherence regarding construction training issues.

Other suggestions for improving the training system in the construction industry have been

- increasing client involvement to insist upon fully-trained workers, thus encouraging employers to train their workforce
- more co-ordination between the training organisations so that the level of training is satisfactory throughout the industry

- organising training schemes to be more in line with the industry's needs at a site level, with more client and employer involvement in the training organisations.

Notes

1. which has developed a modern apprenticeship model framework for the Heating, Ventilating, Air Conditioning, Piping and Domestic Engineering sector.
2. the industry-owned training provider in England and Wales for the electrical installation industry and allied industries
3. SI 1964/1079, and the Industrial Training Act 1982 (as amended by the Employment Act 1989 (s.38))
4. SI 1964/1086, SI 1991/1305, SI 1999/158 and the Industrial Training Act 1982
5. in accordance with the Industrial Training Act 1982
6. see Sections 7.4.1. and 7.4.2. for CITB and ECITB small employer exemptions
7. as defined in SI 1964/1079 and SI 1999/159, and SI 1964/1086, SI 1991/1305, SI 1999/158 and SI 2000/433
8. SI 2000/433
9. as allowed for under s11(3) of the Industrial Training Act 1982
10. i.e. NVQ/SVQ Level 3

8

TUPE and the construction industry

8.1. OVERVIEW

The Transfer of Undertakings (Protection of Employment) Regulations 1981,[1] commonly known by the acronym TUPE, are of major importance to employers in the construction industry. They raise issues where

- a business is transferred (for example, where the business of one contractor is sold to another or where a contractor acquires a number of building contracts from the receiver of an insolvent contractor); or
- where responsibility for the provision of services changes from one contractor to another (for example, where a local authority outsources jobbing maintenance work on its estate of council houses, or where a facilities management contractor wins a tender for the maintenance of a railway network).

The increase in Private Finance Initiative (PFI) projects, facilities management and outsourcing contracts within the industry has resulted in construction companies having to deal with TUPE issues more frequently.

It is important to be able to predict when TUPE will apply and what the consequences of TUPE will be, in order that an appropriate bid may be made for an acquisition target or that contracts for the provision of services can be appropriately priced. It is because the circumstances in which TUPE will apply are so difficult to predict and the legal principles so confused that this area of employment law has become notorious.

8.2. GENERAL PRINCIPLES

TUPE was passed to implement into UK law the European Union Directive[2] 'on the approximation of the laws of Member States relating to the safeguarding of employee rights in the event of transfers of undertakings between businesses or parts of a business', which is more commonly known as the Acquired Rights Directive (the Directive). The policy objective behind the Directive is to protect the rights of employees who work in an 'undertaking' (typically a business or the provision of a service) which is being transferred.

Where TUPE applies, its implications may be summarised as follows

- The contracts of employment of those employees employed in the undertaking immediately before the transfer are transferred by operation of law to the purchaser of the business or the incoming service provider, as if the transferee employer had always been the employer.
- Not only does the transferee employer inherit the contracts of employment of the transferring employees, but also the extent to which these contracts may be changed (even with the consent of all the parties) is strictly limited.
- All rights, duties and liabilities of the transferor employer arising under or in connection with the transferring contracts of employment are transferred to the transferee employer (subject to certain exceptions). The transferee employer becomes liable for the acts and omissions of the transferor

employer, such as arrears of wages or acts of unlawful discrimination.

- Any dismissal of an employee who is affected by the transfer of an undertaking for a reason connected with the transfer will be *automatically* unfair, unless the dismissal was for an 'economic, technical or organisational reason entailing a change in the workforce.'[3]
- An obligation arises to inform and in certain circumstances to consult with the representatives of the employees who may be affected by the transfer of the undertaking.
- Collective agreements and union recognition may transfer.

8.3.   WHEN DOES TUPE APPLY?

Given that if TUPE applies, a number of important employment consequences follow, it is crucial to establish when TUPE applies and when it does not. The generally accepted test of whether there is a transfer of an undertaking is whether

> what has been [transferred] is an economic entity which is still in existence [after the transfer], and this will be apparent from the fact that its operation is actually being continued or has been taken over by the new employer, with the same economic or similar activities.'[4]

This is not an easy test to apply. It is easy to identify an acquisition of a self-standing business as an economic entity capable of a TUPE transfer. Equally, the mere transfer of some items of plant and machinery is not likely, of itself, to constitute an economic entity. Just where the border is crossed between these two extremes, however, is often unclear, particularly where the economic entity is the provision of services.

The question of whether a given set of circumstances amounts to a transfer of an economic entity can only be answered after consideration of all the features of the activity which are being transferred. No one factor is likely to be decisive. Among the factors to be taken into account in this determination are

- the nature of the activity which is the subject of the transfer
- whether tangible assets such as buildings and movable property are to be transferred
- whether intangible assets are to be transferred, and the extent of their value
- whether or not the majority of the employees are to be taken on by the transferee employer post transfer
- whether or not the transferor employer's customers are to be transferred
- the degree of similarity between the activities carried on before and after the transfer
- the period, if any, for which activities are to be suspended on or after the transfer.[5]

It is important to note, in the context of the transfer of construction work, that the transfer of a contract that merely involved the completion of snagging works was held not to be a transfer of a stable economic entity and therefore TUPE did not apply.[6] In that case, the activity concerned was the completion of a subcontract for joinery work on a construction project, the original subcontractor having defaulted. There was held not to be a TUPE transfer to the incoming subcontractor because, come the end of the building project, the undertaking of providing joinery services was to cease.

In the majority of business acquisitions, TUPE will apply because the purchaser of the business is interested in acquiring the 'economic entity' with a view to continuing the enterprise. Where the activity is the delivery of services, however, the position is often less clear. In 1997 there was a material change in the approach of the courts to the transfer of responsibility for the provision of services stemming from the decision of the European Court in the case of *Süzen*. The case concerned the transfer of a cleaning contractor upon retender. According to the Court, for the Directive (and therefore TUPE) to apply, there must be either

- a transfer, from one undertaking to the other, of significant tangible or intangible assets; or
- (in the case of labour intensive undertakings) a transfer of a major part of the workforce, in terms of their numbers and skills, assigned by the outgoing service provider to the performance of the contract.

The consequences of the *Süzen* case[7] are that

(a) there will not be a 'relevant transfer' for the purposes of TUPE merely on the basis of a continuation or assumption of activities

(b) assuming that one or more activity in question is transferred, it will be a matter of fact and degree in every case as to whether the identity of the transferred activity has been retained

(c) where the entity in question is essentially a group of workers carrying out a particular task, unless a major part of that group in terms of their numbers and skills is transferred, an economic entity is unlikely to be considered to have been transferred.

In all other cases, it will be necessary to demonstrate a transfer of 'significant' tangible or intangible assets and that will be a question of fact and degree for an employment tribunal to decide. Of course, whether assets transfer can be determined by the parties to the contract. For example, on the transfer of responsibility for the provision of maintenance services, whether assets such as a parts stock room/workshop, a fleet of vans and software for client interface and work scheduling transfer to the transferee employer is likely to be a key determinant of whether there is a TUPE transfer.

The impact of *Süzen* draws attention to a habitual risk for contractors — a risk they must always seek to lay off or to price. Previously, contractors could reasonably have expected TUPE to have applied in the great majority of contracting-out situations and upon the retendering of services. As a result, contractors accepted the transfer of employees at the start of a contract expecting that the employees would transfer again from the incumbent contractor should they be unsuccessful on retender, with no resultant redundancy liabilities accruing to the contractor. However, if the contractor lost the contract on retendering, and if TUPE no longer applied to transfer the employees to the new contractor following the change in emphasis in the *Süzen* case, contractors feared that they would be faced with substantial redundancy costs.

A degree of order has been restored following the Court of Appeal's decision in *ECM (Vehicle Delivery Services) Ltd* v. *Cox*. In this case, the haulage contractor who won a tender to deliver motor vehicles sought to avoid the application of TUPE by relying strictly on the *Süzen* decision. No significant assets transferred and the incoming contractor refused to employ any staff previously engaged in the provision of those services. The Court held that the importance of the decision in *Süzen* had been 'overstated' and should be viewed 'in its proper context'. The Court insisted that a broad view was taken of the consequences of the award of the contract to an alternative contractor and that all factors be considered. They found that the absence of a transfer of assets or employees, while relevant, was not fatal to the argument that there was, nonetheless, a TUPE transfer. The most important question to ask, according to the Court, was whether the undertaking that had transferred had retained its identity in the hands of the incoming contractor.

Unfortunately, commercial uncertainty has been the inevitable result of a lack of direction shown by the courts. Notwithstanding a contractor's careful consideration of all the factors and having taken legal advice, the position may still be unclear. In many instances, there is a risk that an incoming contractor may suffer an unforeseen transfer of employees. Cost implications are likely to include redundancy liabilities or payroll overheads in excess of what might otherwise have been incurred due to the transfer of historic liabilities. If, as will often be the case, it is simply not clear whether a given set of circumstances give rise to a TUPE transfer, the parties will invariably make assumptions for commercial purposes. It is advisable to underpin those assumptions wherever possible — for example, by pricing the risk of a TUPE transfer into a tender for the provision of services, or by allocating TUPE risks within a contract for the sale and purchase of a business by the use of warranties and indemnities. A properly drafted contract may allow scope for hedging against the vagaries of the law in this area.

8.4. WHO TRANSFERS?

Those employees who are employed in the undertaking or the part of an undertaking immediately before the transfer will become employees of the transferee. Although the transfer operates automatically by operation of law, there is plenty of scope for the transferor to redeploy employees so as to bring them within or take them out of the scope of TUPE.

Should a transferor employer wish to retain the services of an employee who is earmarked for transfer, he could do so by redeploying him so that he is not employed immediately before the transfer in the undertaking which is the subject of the transfer. The converse, a practice known colloquially as 'dumping', involves the transferor employer moving employees into the undertaking at the eleventh hour so that the employees are technically employed in the undertaking which transfers immediately before the transfer, and become employees of the transferee employer. Typically, this practice results in the transferee employer inheriting an overmanned workforce and poor quality employees.

While the courts and tribunals have expressed a distaste for such practices, it is often difficult for a transferee employer to spot and the language of TUPE makes it almost impossible for the transferee employer to seek redress on legal grounds.

A further danger for transferee employers, which hangs on the term 'immediately before', surrounds dismissals prior to the transfer. The courts have held[8] that a dismissal which cannot be said to have taken place immediately before the transfer, in the literal sense of the phrase, but which was occasioned by reason of the transfer (for example, dismissals to make an overmanned business more attractive to a potential purchaser) will be deemed to have been made 'immediately before the transfer' and hence the liabilities associated with these dismissals will transfer to the transferee employer.

Whether an employee can be said to be employed in the undertaking is another area of difficulty, particularly where only a part of an undertaking is being transferred. Employees often will work some of their time on one project and the rest of their time elsewhere within the employer's business. Only those employees who are 'assigned' to the undertaking or part of an undertaking which is being transferred will transfer to the transferee employer.[9]

Take, for example, a situation where a maintenance contractor is responsible for providing a variety of services to the building of a certain client (Client A). The contractor services those buildings from its local depot, which also services a variety of other clients. Client A puts the contract out to retender and the contractor loses. As a consequence, the contractor loses a significant volume of work for the particular depot. If the appointment of a new contractor by Client A amounts to a TUPE transfer, the question to be asked is which employees of the outgoing contractor become employees of the incoming contractor. If a given employee is assigned to work exclusively or principally for Client A, the position is clear. However, if an employee is not assigned exclusively to the work of Client A, but works for a variety of different clients including Client A at different times, to varying degrees, potentially that employee may not transfer and may leave the outgoing contractor with a redundancy liability if he has no other work on which to deploy him. In practice, the assignment test has been stretched to recognise that someone who spends a significant proportion of his time on the work of Client A among a range of other clients may be considered to have been assigned to the transferring service contract. Just what proportion of his time and over what period of time he must have spent on work for Client A to qualify as 'assigned' is not clear. However, the greater the proportion of time, the greater the likelihood that the employee will transfer. Ordinarily an employee must have worked at least 50% of his time on the transferring service contract. The uncertainty surrounding the issue of assignment means that it is often advisable for incoming and outgoing contractors to negotiate and settle which employees are assigned and therefore transfer and which do not; failure to do so can result in an unpredictable dispute before an employment tribunal.

A further point to bear in mind is that in order to transfer, the worker must be an employee (as opposed to an independent contractor) of the transferor. A large construction company will typically have a substantial number of subsidiary companies. Often all the employees within the group will be employed by one service company. Should a subsidiary decide to sell or outsource its business or a part of its business, it is likely that there will be no employees employed by the transferor subsidiary company in the transferring business — hence the employees who ordinarily work in that business do not fall within the protection of TUPE. Much as the courts dislike this loophole,[10] it is there to be exploited.

8.4.1. Can employees refuse to transfer?

Employees who would otherwise transfer have the right to opt out of the transfer.[11] If they do so, however, their employment will terminate without giving rise to a right to claim a redundancy payment or that they have been unfairly dismissed. As there is no transfer, no other employment liabilities (such as non-payment of wages) in respect of that employee will transfer to the transferee employer.[12]

It has been held that an employee's objection to being transferred can be conveyed by word or deed.[13] It was a question of fact in each case whether the employee's state of mind amounted to a withholding of consent to the transfer and whether the state of mind was brought to the attention of the transferor employer.

8.4.2. Transfer of terms and conditions

TUPE provides[14] that 'all the transferor's rights, powers, duties and liabilities under or in connection with the transferring employee's contract of employment are transferred to the transferee'. This all-embracing concept includes rights under the contract of employment, statutory rights, and continuity of employment.

Rights which transfer include the following

Terms and Conditions

Employees become employees of the transferee on the same terms and conditions. To a large extent, it is as if a contract of employment has been pulled from the personnel records and the name of the transferor employer changed to the transferee employer.

Status

The employment relationship is transferred as if the employee had always been employed by the transferee. Hence, any employment benefits that relate to the employee's status would also transfer — for example, holiday entitlement which is calculated by length of service would be calculated on the basis of continuity of service stretching back before the transfer. Equally, seniority is capable of transferring.

Arrears of pay and other liabilities

As there is a transfer of the employment relationship and of all associated liabilities, any contractual arrears will transfer. For example, if there are arrears of pay, outstanding expenses or accrued benefits, such as holiday pay, these will all transfer. Needless to say, it is important for the purchaser of a business to either quantify these outstanding liabilities and to anticipate them when settling on a purchase price or to ensure that the transferor employer provides an indemnity for such liabilities. Ideally, both steps should be taken although the latter will only be appropriate if the transferor is creditworthy for the indemnity. For an incoming contractor with no contract between it and the former provider of services, the position will not be so straightforward although the incoming contractor may be able to secure some protection through its contract with the client.

Statutory claim

Statutory rights will transfer in tandem with the transfer of the employee's terms and conditions. This will mean, for example, that an employee who has been employed by the transferee for only a matter of months may have the right to bring a claim for unfair dismissal against the transferee employer shortly after the transfer because of the aggregation of his pre-transfer service. The date of commencement of continuous service will be the date that applied in relation to employment with the transferor employer.

Restrictive covenants

As contract terms, restrictive covenants will transfer. However, the extent to which they are appropriate to protect the transferee employer's legitimate business interests must be reviewed by the transferee employer. The transferor employer should also bear in mind that he will lose the protection of restrictive covenants, for the benefit of the covenants will transfer to become a contractual benefit for the transferee employer.

Bonuses, profit sharing and share options

These rights are capable of transferring as a matter of theory but, in practice, the conditions that attach to bonuses and profit sharing schemes and the rules of share-option schemes will generally be drafted so that the right to participate in such schemes ceases to exist upon the employee ceasing to be employed by the transferee employer. Furthermore, the criteria for the award of bonuses will have changed by reason of the transfer. In order to avoid a breach of contract, the transferee employer may have to put into place benefits of equivalent value.

Industrial injuries
An industrial injury claim will transfer. Hence, the transferee could find itself liable for substantial claims where, for example, employees were exposed, pre transfer, to a harmful working environment. Particular attention should be given by the transferee employer to insurance cover in respect of such claims, which may have arisen at the time when the transferee did not have insurance in place in respect of these employees. There is caselaw to suggest that in these circumstances reliance may be placed on the transferor's insurance.[15]

The following rights do not transfer.

Pensions
Rights in relation to occupational pension schemes are specifically excluded from the scope of TUPE.[16] The following points, however, should be borne in mind

- It is only rights in relation to occupational pension schemes that do not transfer. If, for example, there was a clause in an employee's contract of employment whereby his employer was obliged to pay 5% of salary into a personal pension plan on behalf of that employee, then such a right would not be a right in relation to an occupational pension scheme and would transfer.

- It is only the provisions of an occupational pension scheme that relate to old age, invalidity or survivors that will not transfer. If, for example, there is a severance benefit scheme built into the pension scheme, then this would transfer. TUPE was written in this way because the Civil Service pension scheme, for example, contains a contractual enhanced benefits on redundancy.

- The Acquired Rights Directive was revised to provide for the transfer of pension rights at the option of Member States. It is believed that the UK Government will utilise this provision to amend TUPE and provide for the transfer of occupational pension scheme rights.

Criminal liability

Vicarious liability
whereby the employer becomes liable for the acts of the employee
done in the course of his employment, does not transfer.

8.4.3.   Changing terms and conditions post transfer

Transferee employers will often wish to harmonise the employment
contracts of the transferring employees with those of their existing
workforce and will often wish to change terms and conditions to tie
performance more closely to remuneration.

However, although it is possible to change terms and conditions
as a matter of general law, such variations are void when they take
place in connection with a TUPE transfer and are detrimental to
the employee. This point was established in the House of Lords'
decision in the cases of *Wilson v. St. Helens Borough Council* and
Meade & Baxendale v. British Fuels Ltd. The practical implications
of the decision can be summarised as follows.

(a) Even where employees had expressly agreed to a variation of
    their employment contracts, it did *not* bind the employees
    where that variation was detrimental to the employees, and
    connected to the transfer.

    In other words, the employee was able to rely on the terms
    and conditions he had enjoyed prior to the transfer even after
    he had agreed to a variation with the transferee employer. The
    conclusion follows the principle that an employee is unable to
    delegate from his or her rights under TUPE, even by
    agreement. The House of Lords agreed with the Employment
    Appeal Tribunal (EAT's) analysis of the Court of Justice of the
    European Communities (ECJ's) decision in *Foreningen af
    Arbejdsledere I. Danmark v. Daddy's Dance Hall A/S.*

(b) The Court of Appeal had been wrong to consider the validity
    of the variation in the employees' contracts by looking at
    whether there had been an 'effective' dismissal and re-

engagement of the employees on the new terms of employment. The Court of Appeal had been wrong in finding that the dismissal was only valid if there had been an economic technical or organisational ('ETO') reason for the dismissal.

(c) However, where there is no dismissal but merely a variation of the employee's contract, the finding at point (a) above applies.

This clarification, while it is to be welcomed, leaves a number of issues outstanding. Unfortunately, the House of Lords did not give more than the briefest of guidance on the crucial point of when a variation will be connected to a transfer so as to make it potentially void. How long does a transferee employer have to wait to show a change is no longer connected with the transfer? Is it merely a question of time? What factors are determinative of this issue? On this point, considerable confusion still exists as the matter, according to the House of Lords, must be determined by the employment tribunal based on the particular circumstances of the case. Practically, it appears that employers seeking to harmonise their employees' terms and conditions are only able to do so to the extent that each party is prepared to adhere to the bargain. Unfortunately, the employees are able to re-open their contracts of employment up to six years after the alleged variation. Employers, when considering harmonisation, should take steps to establish that the reasons for the variation are not connected to the transfer. For example, they could argue that the variations were due to advances in technology; or in line with the employer's continuing group-wide review of all its contracts. Unfortunately, however ingenious these arguments may be, it must be recognised that an employment tribunal or court may still find that the underlying reason was the transfer and that the variations are therefore void.

8.4.4. Transfer-connected dismissals

Dismissals connected with a transfer are subject to the presumption that they are automatically unfair unless they are for economic, technical or organisational reasons entailing a change in the workforce. Even if a dismissal is not subject to the presumption that it is unfair, it may nevertheless be found to be unfair under general principles.

If a dismissal is found to be unfair, liability will transfer to the transferee who will be liable for any unfair dismissal award. Therefore it is essential for the transferee to consider before dismissing any employees

- whether the reason for dismissal is connected with the transfer.
- if so, is the ETO defence available?
- if so, will the dismissal be fair in any event?

It has been held[17] that an employer, to claim an ETO defence, must show that it plans to change the numbers or functions of the employees looked at as a whole. An ETO defence will not be available if a planned harmonisation does not involve changes in numbers or functions of the workforce as it will not 'entail changes in the workforce'. However, a redundancy programme following a transfer will generally provide a transferee employer with an ETO defence since it involves a reduction in the numbers of employees required to carry out work of a particular kind.

As stated above, if the transferee is able to show an ETO defence or if the dismissal was not connected to the transfer, the general principles of fairness apply.[18] If there are redundancies to be made, the transferee must follow a fair procedure in adequately consulting with the employees (and their representatives) and selecting fairly the employees to be dismissed. With this in mind, a transferee should be particularly concerned to clarify whether it has inherited any contractual redundancy procedure from the transferor which may have to be followed, as well as whether there are any enhanced redundancy terms which transfer.

8.5. INFORMATION AND CONSULTATION

See accompanying box for a checklist of a transferor's responsibilities to inform and consult under Regulations 10 and 11 of TUPE.

Checklist of transferor's responsibilities to inform and consult under regulations 10 and 11 of TUPE

1. Identify which employees are 'affected employees'. These are employees who regardless of whether they are likely to transfer or not — may be affected by the transfer or may be affected by measures taken in connection with the transfer.

2. Identify, in respect of each description of affected employee, who are the appropriate representatives of those affected employees. These may be

   - representatives of an independent trade union recognised by the employer; or
   - representatives already elected for other purposes who have authority to act in this capacity, bearing in mind the purposes for which they were elected; or
   - representatives elected by the employees for this purpose in an election which the employer must facilitate.

3. The employer has an obligation to inform and almost certainly also to consult the 'appropriate representatives' of all affected employees employed by the employer. Define the category of affected employees who are represented by the recognised union. The union representatives will be the appropriate representatives for these purposes. If there are other affected employees who are outside the category of employees in respect of which the union is recognised, consider who the appropriate representatives are for those employees.

4. On the basis that the employer does not recognise a trade union in respect of any given description of affected employee, identify whether there are any appointed/ elected employee representatives already in place for other purposes (e.g. a staff council) who it would be appropriate to inform and to consult with in relation to

this category of employee. If there are any such representatives already in place, it is the employer's choice whether he deems them to be the appropriate representatives for the purposes of this TUPE information and consultation exercise or whether his employer uses the method in paragraph 5. below to select alternative representatives.

5. If there are no existing representatives identified under paragraph 4. in respect of a particular description of employee or if the employer would prefer to have new representatives elected (and assuming that the employees concerned are prepared to participate in electing new representatives) an election should be held for the specific purposes of appointing representatives for this TUPE exercise. The following steps should be taken

- It is the responsibility of the employer to run the election. The employer must make such arrangements as are 'reasonably practical' to ensure that the election is fair. Consider how this can best be achieved — make sure that every affected employee has written notice of how the election procedure is to be conducted; give clear instructions as to what candidates need to do to put themselves forward; ensure that the ballot is a secret ballot; take steps to ensure that employees are not concerned about being in any way open to a detriment by reason of participating.

- The employer must determine how many representatives should be elected. There must be enough to represent all the affected employees, ensuring that there is at least one representative in respect of each class of employee. A minimum of three to four is advisable. Decide whether the consultation exercise can go ahead as one exercise or whether it is necessary to consult with different categories of employees separately.

- Determine the term of office of the representatives and ensure that it is long enough to last at least until the transfer has taken place.
- Candidates must be affected employees. Only affected employees can vote. An employee should have a number of votes equivalent to the number of representatives to be elected (or, where he is a member of a particular class, a number of votes equivalent to the number of representatives to be elected in respect of that particular class).

6. If in respect of a particular description of employee there are no trade unions, no representatives already in place who would be suitable, and the affected employees failed to appoint representatives within a 'reasonable time', the employer's obligations are limited to circulating the information which would have been given to the representatives (see paragraph 7.) to all affected employees in that description of employee. It is difficult to give guidance on what would be a reasonable time. It should be at least a week and it would be appropriate to point out in the initial circular to employees the time-scale within which candidates must come forward.

7. When representatives have been identified, the necessary information should be given to them. This is

- the fact that the relevant transfer is to take place, when, approximately it is to take place and the reasons for it
- the legal, economic and social implications of the transfer for the affected employees
- the measures which the employer envisages it will, in connection with the transfer, take in relation to those employees or, if the employer envisages that no measures will be taken, say so

- The measures which the transferee envisages it will take in connection with the transfer in respect of transferring employees or, if none are envisaged, say so.

8. The employer should serve a formal request on the transferee asking the transferee to let the employer have the information necessary to enable compliance with the fourth bullet point in 7. above. They have a legal obligation to do so.

9. The information must be given long enough before the transfer to enable consultation between the employer and the appropriate representatives of the affected employees to take place. Consultation is only necessary where measures are envisaged — in the event that no measures are envisaged in respect of affected employees of a particular description, there is no need to consult in relation to those employees and, therefore, the information may be conveyed only shortly prior to the transfer if the employer chooses to delay. Information must be given in writing. In the case of a union, it must be posted to the address of its head or main office.

10. Consultation must be entered into with a view to seeking the agreement of the representatives to the measures which are proposed. Representations of the representatives must be considered by the employer and a reply must be given, with reasons where the representations are rejected.

TUPE imposes obligations on both the transferor and the transferee employer to inform and in certain circumstances to consult with representatives of the employees who may be affected by the transfer in relation to the proposed transfer and its implications. The consultation must be meaningful, must seek to achieve agreement, and must take place in 'good time' before the transfer to allow for proper consultation.

Failure to inform or to consult in accordance with Regulation 10 of TUPE can result in protective awards being

payable to each employee in respect of where there is a
failure, which can be as high as 13 weeks' pay for each
employee.

8.5.1. Transfer of trade union recognition

Where the undertaking which has been transferred maintains its
distinct identity post transfer, then trade union recognition rights
are capable of being transferred to the transferee employer. Where
an independent trade union is recognised by the transferor
employer in respect of employees who become employees of the
transferee employer by operation of TUPE, then the transferee
employer shall be deemed to have recognised the union to the same
extent as recognition was granted by the transferor employer.[19]

8.5.2. Transfer of collective agreements

Collective agreements relating to transferring employees transfer
provided that

- at the time of the transfer, there is a collective agreement in
  place
- they have been made by or on behalf of the transferor (that is
  to say that it would encompass a collective agreement where
  the transferor participates through a trade association)
- a trade union is recognised by the transferor in respect of any
  employee whose contract transfers to the transferee by reason
  of the application of Regulation 5 of TUPE[20]

and in such circumstances that collective agreement applies in
relation to that employee as if made by the transferee with the union.

8.5.3. Protection in a TUPE situation

The prospect of a TUPE transfer brings with it the risk of
transferring staff and liabilities which the transferee must accept

and plan for (such as pricing in the consequence of higher payroll costs than would be incurred if employees were recruited on the open market) or protection should be sought in the form of an indemnity. While this may be achievable in the context of an acquisition, on a transfer of service providers there will often be no contract between the outgoing and incoming service providers. Hence, it becomes necessary for the incoming service provider to look to the client for protection. The client, in turn, should anticipate this situation when drafting the contract for services to ensure that the client and its subsequent subcontractors are protected against the transfer of liability.

Likewise, if there is no transfer of employees at the end of a contract period, a contractor will be faced with the prospect of significant redundancy liabilities. In these circumstances it is necessary to price in the risk or to lay off some of the risk by the contract with the client, for example by ensuring that retenders will be made on the basis that all tenderers will be obliged to offer employment on like terms to the employees of the contractor if successful.

NOTES

1. SI 1981/1794
2. 77/187/EEC
3. although see *Kerry Foods v. Creber*
4. *Spijkers v. Gebroeders Benedik Abbatoir*
5. *Rygaard v. Strö Mölle Akustik*
6. examples as set out in *Spijkers*
7. as interpreted by the Court of Appeal in the case of *Betts v. Brintel Helicopters Ltd and KLM ERA Helicopters (UK) Ltd*
8. *Litster v. Forth Dry Docks & Engineering Co. Ltd*
9. *Botzen Rotterdamsche Droogdok Maatschappij BV*
10. see *Duncan Web Offset (Maidstone) Ltd v. Cooper*
11. Regulation 5(4)
12. But see *University of Oxford v. Humphreys*

13. *Hay v. George Hanson (Building Contractors) Ltd*
14. Regulation 5(1)
15. *Pall Mall v. Bernadone*
16. Regulation 7
17. *Berriman v. Delabole Slate Ltd*
18. under Section 98(4) of the Employment Rights Act 1996
19. Regulation 9
20. Regulation 6

Table of statutes and European directives

Table of statutory instruments and orders

Employment Rights (Increase of Limits) Order 1999 (SI 1999/ 3375)

Guarantee Payments (Exemption) (No 1) Order 1977 (SI 1977/ 156)

Guarantee Payments (Exemption) (No 30) Order 1996 (SI 1996/ 2132)

Income Tax (Sub-contractors in the Construction Industry) (Amendment) Regulations 1998 (SI 1998/2622)

Industrial Training (Construction Board) Order 1964 (SI 1964/ 1079)

Industrial Training (Engineering Board) Order 1964 (SI 1964/ 1086)

Industrial Training (Engineering Construction Board) Order 1991 (SI 1991/1305)

Industrial Training Levy (Construction Board) Order 1999 (SI 1999/159)

Industrial Training Levy (Engineering Construction Board) Order 1999 (SI 1999/158)

Industrial Training Levy (Engineering Construction Board) Order 2000 (SI 2000/433)

Maternity and Parental Leave etc. Regulations 1999 (SI 1999/ 3312)

National Minimum Wage Regulations 1999 (SI 1999/584)

Part-time Workers (Prevention of Less Favourable Treatment) Regulations 2000 (to be in force on 1 July 2000)

Transfer of Undertakings (Protection of Employment) Regulations 1981 (SI 1981/1794)

Working Time Regulations 1998 (SI 1998/1833)

Working Time Regulations 1999 (SI 1999/3372)

Table of cases

Useful sources

ACAS	www.acas.org.uk
AEEU	www.aeeu.org.uk
B&CE	www.bandce.org.uk
Building Magazine	www.building-focus.co.uk
CBI	www.cbi.org.uk
CITB	www.citb.org.uk
Civil Engineering Contractors Association	www.ceca.co.uk
Construction Confederation	www.constructionconfederation.co.uk
Construction Industry Board	www.ciboard.org.uk
Construction News	www.cnplus.co.uk
Department of Trade and Industry	www.dti.gov.uk
DETR	www.detr.gov.uk
ECITB	www.ecitb.org.uk
Electrical Contractors Association	www.eca.co.uk
European Union	europe.eu.int
GMB	www.gmb.org.uk

Government Information Service	www.open.gov.uk
Health and Safety Executive	www.hse.gov.uk/hsehome.htm
Heating and Ventilating Contractors Association	www.hvca.org.uk
HM Treasury	www.hm-treasury.gov.uk
Inland Revenue	www.inlandrevenue.gov.uk
Institution of Civil Engineers	www.ice.org.uk
Joint Industry Board for the Electrical Contracting Industry	www.jib.org.uk
Masons	www.masons.com
National Federation of Builders	www.builders.org.uk
Royal Institute of Chartered Surveyors	www.rics.org.uk
Society of Construction Law	www.scl.org.uk
TGWU	www.tgwu.org.uk
Thomas Telford	www.t-telford.co.uk
Trade Union Congress (TUC)	www.tuc.org.uk
Treasury Taskforce	www.treasury-projects-taskforce.gov.uk
UCATT	www.ucatt.org.uk
UK Parliament	www.parliament.the-stationary-office.co.uk

Bibliography & further reading

Advice to sub-contractors going onto deduction under the Construction Industry Scheme (IR164(CIS))

Are your workers employed or self-employed? A Guide for tax and National Insurance for contractors in the construction industry. (IR148/CA69)

Business Transfers and Employee Rights. John McMullen (Butterworths 1998)

Butterworths Employment Law Handbook. Peter Wallington (Butterworths 1999)

Construction Industry: Conditions for getting a sub-contractor's tax certificate (IR40 and IR40(CIS))

Construction industry deduction scheme (IR14/15)

The Construction Industry Scheme (CIS) (CIS Fact 5)

Construction Industry Scheme (IR14/15(CIS))

Contracts of Employment: Law & Practice. Robert Upex and Vivien Shrubsall (FT Law & Tax 1997)

Countering avoidance in the provision of personal services (IR35)

Disability Discrimination Code of Practice (HMSO 1996)

Drafting Contracts of Employment. Gillian Howard (Tolleys 1993)

Employed or self-employed? A guide for tax and National Insurance (IR56/N139)

Employer compliance reviews and negotiations (IR109)

Employment Covenants and Confidential Information: Law, Practice and Technic. Kate Brearley and Selwyn Bloch (Butterworths 1993)

Employment Handbook. Elizabeth Slade QC (Tolleys Employment Service 1999)

Employment Law Aspects of Mergers and Acquisitions: A Practical Guide. Michael Ryley (Hawksmere 1997)

Employment Law Service (Jordans/Institute of Personnel and Development 1998 and updates)

Encyclopedia of Employment Law (Sweet & Maxwell 1998 and updates)

A guide for contractors with registration cards (IR117(CIS))

A guide for sub-contractors for tax certificates (IR116 and IR 116(CIS))

A Guide to the Employment Relations Act 1999. Nicholas Randall and Ian Smith (Butterworths 1999)

Harvey on Industrial Relations and Employment Law (Butterworths 2000 and updates)

Investigations. The examination of business accounts (IR72)

Masons' Guide: Health & Safety Law for the Construction Industry. Susan Fink (Thomas Telford 1997)

Mead's Unfair Dismissal. Michael Rich and Ian Edwards (Longman 1994)

National Insurance for agencies and people finding work through agencies (CA25)

Pay As You Earn (IR34)

Redgraves Health & Safety. John Hendy and Michael Ford (Butterworths 1998)

Sex Discrimination in Employment: Law, Practice and Policy. Richard Townshend-Smith (Sweet & Maxwell 1989)

Staff Transfers in the Public Sector — Statement of Practice (Cabinet Office January 2000)

A sub-contractors guide to the deduction scheme (IR117)

Taking Responsibility: Making Training Work in Construction (Construction Confederation)

TUPE and the Acquired Rights Directive. John Sharland and Stuart Isaacs QC (Trenton Publishing 1996)

Index

153